CASCADIA

A TALE OF TWO CITIES

C A S C

A TALE OF TWO CITIES
SEATTLE AND VANCOUVER, B.C.

Essays by

J. Kingston Pierce

Jim Sutherland

David M. Buerge

Rick Anderson

Roger Downey

Daphne Bramham

Laurel Wellman

Brenda Peterson

A D I A

PHOTOGRAPHS BY MORTON BEEBE

Captions by Morton Beebe and J. Kingston Pierce

HARRY N. ABRAMS, INC., PUBLISHERS

Editors: Sarah Burns and Lory Frankel
Art Director: Samuel N. Antupit
Designer: Liz Trovato
Photo Editor: Meg McVey

Library of Congress Cataloging-in-Publication Data
Beebe, Morton.
Cascadia : a tale of two cities, Seattle and Vancouver, B.C. /
photographs by Morton Beebe ; essays by J. Kingston Pierce…[et al.].
p.   cm.
ISBN 0–8109–4048–5 (clothbound)/ISBN 0–8109–2665–2 (pbk.)
1. Seattle (Wash.)—Pictorial works.   2. Vancouver (B.C.)—
Pictorial works.   3. Seattle (Wash.)—Description and travel.
4. Seattle Region (Wash.)—Description and travel.   5. Vancouver
(B.C.)—Description and travel.   6. Vancouver Region (B.C.)—
Description and travel.   I. Pierce, J. Kingston, 1957–.
II. Title.
F899.S443.B43   1996
979.5–dc20   96–11525

Published in 1996 by Harry N. Abrams, Incorporated, New York
A Times Mirror Company

Printed and bound in Japan

Endpapers:
Satellite image of Cascadia. Seattle satellite image provided by TerraNOVA International,
Los Altos, California

Page 1:
American and Canadian flags fly over the Hotel de Haro on San Juan Island, Washington, during
the Fourth of July celebration.

Pages 2–3:
Boats pass through the Lake Washington Ship Canal in this view looking east from Seattle's
Mountlake Bridge toward the Cascade Mountains.

Pages 4–5:
Canada Place, Vancouver's convention and visitors' center, built as part of Expo '86, features
canvas and metal structures reminiscent of ships' sails.

Pages 6–7:
Orcas, or killer whales, swim in Haro Strait near the United States–Canada border.
Photograph by Kelley Balcomb-Bartok

CONTENTS

PREFACE AND ACKNOWLEDGMENTS

While on a cross-country skiing assignment in 1972, I ventured north to a remote British Columbia community known for its weekend ski activity—Whistler, a resort that was open only between October and May. During my visit, I fell in love with a shoreline cabin on nearby Alta Lake, from which I could study the towering Cascade peaks and listen to the sounds of the steam-driven trains chugging between mountains. I reveled in the comforting isolation of that spot. Coming from busy San Francisco, the Pacific Northwest backwoods seemed like a place so far out of the mainstream that even your private demons couldn't find you. It was hard back then to take seriously the predictions of Canadian Olympic skier Nancy Greene, who told me that if it was developed imaginatively, the Whistler-Blackcomb area might compete with Aspen and Sun Valley. Come on, I thought, you're dreaming!

A decade later, after selling my lakeside retreat, I returned to what had been the "village" of Whistler—and was stunned by the elegant, high-rise ski lodges and year-round sports centers, thronged by thousands of international visitors. Our cozy retreat had been discovered.

Something similar has happened to the two putative capitals of the Northwest: Seattle, Washington, and Vancouver, British Columbia. World's fairs in both cities have focused international attention here. Visitors now come from as far away as Berlin and Beijing to walk this region's forests, fish its rivers, and dine in its fine restaurants. At the same time, the residents are working together and proposing such things as a cross-border Olympics and streamlining the traffic flow across the United States–Canadian boundary. Visually, the border is a magnificent Peace Arch Park, a site of weddings and picnics.

Italy's Ambassador Bruno Biancheri, writing for the *New York Times*, observed that the center of power has always drifted from east to west and prophesied that the power center will thrust its roots not in California but in the Pacific Northwest, by melding with the Asian world in an entirely new and potent way. Sitting on Seattle's waterfront looking at the blond and dark-haired youth mingling, he felt that here, just here, the present meets the future.

Over a period of three years, I have tried to capture on film the features and the life-style of Cascadia, while eight of the region's finest writers have offered descriptions in words. Together, words and pictures offer an unparalleled portrait, past, present, and future, of a vital and unique region.

PEACE ARCH PARK, CREATED IN 1921 BY SAM HILL, A WASHINGTON PROMOTER OF GOOD HIGHWAYS AND GOOD INTERNATIONAL RELATIONS, LIES AT THE BORDER OF THE UNITED STATES AND CANADA.
RIGHT:
LOOKING FROM THE UNITED STATES TO CANADA.
FAR RIGHT:
LOOKING FROM CANADA TO THE UNITED STATES.

This book would not have been possible without the hospitality, support, interest, and kindness of the following: Gil and Pam Powers, who initiated my visual interest in the region and remained my mentors; Bob Sung, who provided insight and guidance to the growing Vancouver Chinese population; J. Kingston Pierce, who introduced me to the writers' communities in both Seattle and Vancouver; Ron and Barbara Howard, who shared the ski slopes of Whistler; Paul Schell and Bruce Agnew, pioneering economic relations across borders; Andrew Saxton and family, aboard the *Saxony*, who led me along the British Columbia waters; David Hughbanks, Jane Milholland, and Vi Mar, my guides in their communities; John Creighton, Jr., at Weyerhaeuser, and Phil Condit, at Boeing, for providing historical perspectives; the archivists at Seattle's Museum of History and Industry, for their help in researching obscure photographs from Seattle's past; B. J. Stokey, at the Port of Seattle, for believing in the project; Mary Louise Harris, at Image Bank, for her good editor's eyes; Harold Sund and Bob Peterson, for generously sharing their photographers' insights of the region; Doug Rowan and Charles Mauzy, at Corbis; Val and Ira Kaye, Jim Durst, Betsy and Les Gunther, Paul and Glenda Barrett, Pat and John Davis, Kathy and Doug Raff, Nan and Paul Woolridge, Louise and Ned Kurabi for their hospitality; Sam Antiput, Abrams book designer, who made the project exciting by sharing his enthusiasm for the book; Tom Bachand, who kept my San Francisco office going during my long journeys into Cascadia; Eastman Kodak, which generously kept my film supply going; and Danielle Chavanon, my tireless companion.

Morton Beebe

WHERE IN THE WORLD IS CASCADIA?

J. Kingston Pierce

AERIAL VIEW OVER THE
STRAIT OF JUAN DE
FUCA CROSSING THE
UNITED STATES–
CANADA BORDER.

It would be difficult—probably impossible—to identify a time when residents of America's Pacific Northwest and the southwestern corner of Canada were completely content with their political borders. History offers up a lengthy menu of actual and proposed changes.

During the early nineteenth century, the powerful British Hudson's Bay Company lorded over what are now the province of British Columbia and the state of Washington. A boundary compromise dividing Canada from the northwestern United States wasn't settled until 1846, and it took another seven years for Washington to win independence from the vast Oregon Territory (originally encompassing not only present-day Oregon but also southern British Columbia, Washington, Idaho, and western Montana). Ever since, Americans and British Columbians, dissatisfied with national rule from afar, have sought to recarve this wet, wooded quarter, advocating the creation of new cantons called Jefferson or Columbia or Siskiyou, all of which they claim would make better sense than the existing subdivisions.

The more recent idea of establishing a binational domain called "Cascadia"—spreading out from the Seattle–Vancouver, B.C., corridor to take in all of the old Oregon Territory, plus Alberta and Alaska—might seem to smack of the same provinciality that has permeated previous boundary-jiggering schemes. This time, however, supporters are galvanized by such issues as commerce, transportation, and environmental concerns, all related to growth as much as governance.

"There is no desire to unify the region politically, nor to homogenize the historic cultures of either Canada or the United States," assure Paul Schell and John Hamer, leading members of the Discovery Institute, a Seattle-based group that touts cross-border connections throughout the Northwest and western Canada. "What inspires is not a marriage, but a partnership...."

If it could be achieved, this partnership might eventually wield significant influence. Consider that Cascadia (named after the rugged Cascade Mountains, which march north from California into lower British Columbia) is greater in area than the European Community, with an annual gross domestic production that ranks it as the world's tenth-largest economy. With one of the ten top port systems in the world, Cascadia seems destined to play an increasingly vital role in Pacific Rim trade—a fact acknowledged by President Bill Clinton, who chose Seattle as the site for a historic 1993 meeting of leaders from nations that compose the Asia-Pacific Economic Cooperation (APEC) forum.

Some six million people live along the culture- and business-rich umbilical linking Seattle with Vancouver—more people than call either the Washington, D.C., or Boston metropolises home. The world's biggest aerospace enterprise and America's number-one exporter, the Boeing Company, is headquartered here. So are mining mammoths on the order of Cominco, forestry enterprises like Weyerhaeuser and MacMillan Bloedel, and major life-style arbiters such as Nordstrom (the high-end clothing chain) and Starbucks Coffee (responsible for giving most of North America a caffeine high). More than a thousand computer software ventures—including billionaire Bill Gates's Microsoft—have helped make this international region third among the continent's software development tracts. Vancouver, with the third-largest metropolitan population in Canada (after those of Toronto and Montreal), is fast becoming "Hollywood North"—or "Brollywood," as some call it, alluding to a British slang term for umbrella. The city's burgeoning local television and filmmaking industry pumps almost half a billion Canadian dollars into the British Columbia economy every year, and Vancouver has stood in admirably on the screen for such diverse locales as New York, San Francisco, Hong Kong, and London.

Already there have been some prominent and promising signs of Cascadian cooperation.

Trade between Washington and British Columbia has risen rapidly—up 50 percent just between 1991 and 1994. There's talk of constructing a high-speed rail connection from Vancouver, B.C., to Eugene, Oregon, and of cooperative agreements between the region's airports and seaports. Environmentalists are striving to create a cross-border Cascades International Park, which would place 1.05 million acres (424,000 hectares) of public lands in the North Cascades ecosystem under joint United States–Canadian management. More than 40 percent of the money needed to operate Seattle's public television station, KCTS, is currently contributed by Vancouverites. Shared concerns over salmon habitats, water and air pollution, and the fast-declining timber industry have brought Canadians and American Northwesterners together in constructive debate.

Tourism authorities have even been pushing Seattle and Vancouver—a mere 140 miles, or 225 kilometers, apart—as destinations that can both be appreciated during a single vacation. (For a longer holiday, tourists could also visit the very British city of Victoria, located at the southern end of Vancouver Island and easily accessible by ferry.) This idea works because while these two cities share some historical mileposts and skyline values, they each claim distinctive textures and attractions.

Vancouver is generally the brasher, more energetic, and more visionary of the pair. Founded by mavericks, it has rarely been short of eccentricities. During the 1960s, for instance, Vancouver hired an official Town Fool, and some of its landmarks have clearly been dedicated with more humor than hubris. (Where else but on the south bank of False Creek could you find a place called Leg-in-Boot Square, honoring the sole remains of a pioneer who set off one day on a fifteen-mile trek through the bush to New Westminster?) Although the city has become rather cynical of late, spoiled by many deep-pocketed immigrants from Hong Kong who have biased the inhabitants toward receiving the moneyed masses over the merely huddled ones, its people have at least accepted the fact that Vancouver is an increasingly Asian town.

Like their Seattle neighbors on Puget Sound, Vancouverites are an exercise-inclined people, devoting their weekends to skiing or sea kayaking and skipping power lunches to run along the nearest waterfront. Both populations shy from the pin-striped business armor of Toronto or Manhattan. The alternative on Vancouver and Seattle sidewalks is very casual, with Vancouverites opting for a somewhat trendier look. Warm, sunny days (all too rare in these parts) bring out an even more individualistic breed of Canadian: the nudists who frequent Wreck Beach, near the University of British Columbia campus, with their striped towels and oversized bottles of sunscreen.

Seattle, built principally by puritanical New Englanders and stoic Scandinavians, tends toward less exhibitionism than does Vancouver. Resembling that legendary Cascadian forest giant, Bigfoot, its residents covet their privacy. If Seattleites aren't nearly so sophisticated as they'd like to believe, they have at least been more forward-thinking than many outsiders realize. After all, they established an extensive public parks system early in the twentieth century and more recently created a convenient curbside recycling program that has become a model for other American cities. Yet inciting Seattleites to action is sometimes tough. Decades after they began considering a rapid-transit system, they continue to vote down all such plans…but then complain about local freeway congestion, which now rivals that of Los Angeles.

It's said that Vancouver has style, while Seattle has soul. That may be, but all that soul appears not to have given Washington's foremost city self-confidence. It hungers blatantly for recognition from Eastern tastemakers. This causes some consternation among its artists and architects, who may be passed over in favor of talents boasting national or international credits. At the same time, however, the city's need to affirm its wisdom and evolution has led it to preserve much of its impressive architectural heritage. Visitors can roam the eighty-eight refurbished acres of Pioneer Square, Seattle's original core, full of Richardsonian Romanesque buildings that rose after a devastating fire in 1889 and now house chic coffeehouses, bookstores, and restaurants. Or they can browse through Pike Place Market, a rambling hive of shops established in 1907 at the opposite end of downtown, where crowds paw over handcrafted trinkets and fresh produce or watch as fishmongers fling flounders over the heads of amazed Midwesterners.

Still, the question remains: Can the synergy already so important to Vancouver and Seattle be extended as far north as the Arctic Ocean, as far south as the Oregon–California border, and east into Big Sky country? It will depend on whether the states and provinces crafting the Cascadian dream can subordinate their individual ambitions to a roster of specific superregional goals.

Mark Hatfield, a longtime United States senator from Oregon, sounded hopeful—and anxious to move ahead—when he remarked, "We don't have to agree on everything to work together on anything."

OVERLEAF:
SUNRISE AT FALSE BAY, ON WASHINGTON'S SAN JUAN ISLAND, PROVIDES A QUIET AND LIGHTLY FOGGY OPPORTUNITY TO EXPLORE. PORTLAND FAIR RIDGE IS IN THE BACKGROUND.

THE ISLANDS OF
WASHINGTON'S SAN
JUAN ARCHIPELAGO ARE
THICK WITH OAK-PINE
FORESTS, HAWKS,
SQUIRRELS, AND TIDE
POOLS WHERE SMALL
WATER CREATURES
SECRETE THEMSELVES.
OPPOSITE:
AS THE SUN RISES
OVER SAN JUAN
ISLAND, IT REVEALS
GLACIAL ERRATIC
STONES SCATTERED
OVER A BEACH.
RIGHT:
MOSSES THRIVE IN
THE ISLANDS' COOL
ENVIRONMENT.

IT DOESN'T TAKE A
NATURALIST'S EYE TO
SEE CURIOUS AND
COLORFUL FLORA
SPROUTING OVER SAN
JUAN ISLAND—JUST
CURIOSITY.
ABOVE:
THE BRITTLE PEAR
CACTUS (*OPUNTIA
FRAGILIS*) BLOOMS
YELLOW AND GROWS UP
TO 6 INCHES HIGH
AROUND THE TOWN OF
FRIDAY HARBOR.
BELOW:
MOSSES COME IN JUST
ABOUT EVERY SHADE OF
GREEN IMAGINABLE.

OPPOSITE:
EVEN AT HIGHER
ELEVATIONS, SUCH AS
ARTIST RIDGE ON
WASHINGTON'S MOUNT
BAKER, AN ABUNDANCE
OF FLOWERS AND
OTHER VEGETATION
GREETS THE VISITOR.

OVERLEAF:
THE ENCROACHMENT OF
POWER LINES SEEMS
SACRILEGEOUS AT
BRITISH COLUMBIA'S
ALTA LAKE, WHERE
MOUNT SPROAT (FAR
LEFT) AND RAINBOW
MOUNTAIN REACH
UP TO TICKLE THE
HEAVENS.

STAWAMUS CHIEF,
A 2,140-FOOT
(650-METER) GRANITE
BEHEMOTH JUST
OUTSIDE OF SQUAMISH,
BRITISH COLUMBIA,
LOOMS OVER THE
SQUAMISH HIGHWAY
AND ATTRACTS
CLIMBERS FROM EVERY
CORNER OF THE GLOBE.
EVEN NONCLIMBERS
CAN APPRECIATE ITS
BREEZY HEIGHTS
BY HIKING UP BACK
TRAILS TO STAWAMUS'S
THREE SUMMITS.

OPPOSITE:
EVEN THE WATERFALLS
HERE SEEM WILDLY OUT
OF SCALE. THE *MV
SAXONY* CRUISES PAST
CHATTERBOX FALLS
IN PRINCESS LOUISA
INLET, WHICH ADJOINS
THE MALASPINA STRAIT,
OUTSIDE OF POWELL
RIVER, BRITISH
COLUMBIA.

There are times when Cascadians ask themselves, "What must this place have been like before white settlers arrived?" And then they look around and realize that, in some areas, not much has changed.
ABOVE:
Tulip farms have filled up Washington's Skagit Valley. But Mount Baker in the distance still looks much as it must have when 3d Lt. Joseph Baker, who sailed with British navigator Captain George Vancouver on his 1792 visit to the Pacific Northwest, first saw the peak—and gave his name to it.
BELOW:
The rocky coastline around Friday Harbor, on Washington's San Juan Island, seems untouched by human hands.
OPPOSITE:
Lupine punctuates the predominantly green blanket stretching out around Mount Baker.

OVERLEAF:
Sea kayaks pass the intimidating cliffs of Deception Pass, at the north end of Washington's Whidbey Island. The landmark was named by Captain George Vancouver, who in 1792 mistook it for the entrance to a new bay.

NORTH CASCADES NATIONAL PARK, AT THE BORDER OF CANADA AND THE UNITED STATES, SHOWS OFF ITS MANY PEAKS TO HIGHWAY DRIVERS. HOWEVER, MOST OF IT IS ACCESSIBLE ONLY ON FOOT OR BY SLOWER MEANS OF TRAVEL, SUCH AS BOATS.
OPPOSITE:
CANOEISTS HEAD DOWN THE SKAGIT RIVER, WHICH BORDERS THE PARK AND HOSTS HUNDREDS OF BALD EAGLES EVERY WINTER.
RIGHT:
A THICK SHINGLING OF CLOUDS FINALLY BREAKS OPEN, LETTING THE SUN SHINE THROUGH AGAIN ON THE PARK, NEAR DIABLO LAKE DAM, JUST OFF HIGHWAY 20, IN WASHINGTON.

OVERLEAF:
GUESTS AT THE STATES INN BED AND BREAKFAST (ORIGINALLY CALLED THE BLAZING TREE RANCH) ON SAN JUAN ISLAND CAN ESCAPE THEIR ROOMS TO READ BESIDE A QUIET NEARBY LAKE.

STILLNESS COVERS
CASCADIA AS THE SUN
DIPS BENEATH THE
HORIZON.
OPPOSITE:
LOOKING OVER
MOSQUITO PASS,
TOWARD HENRY ISLAND
IN WASHINGTON'S SAN
JUAN ARCHIPELAGO:
THE SUNSET SEEMS TO
HIGHLIGHT EVERY
RIPPLE OF WATER.
RIGHT:
POPCORN CLOUDS OVER
SEATTLE'S LAKE UNION
RECEIVE THE LAST BITS
OF SUNSHINE.

ABOVE:
SUNSET ON WASHINGTON'S AGATE PASSAGE, WITH THE OLYMPIC MOUNTAINS SHOWING THEIR JAGGED PROFILE IN THE BACKGROUND.

BELOW:
ROWERS HEAD HOME AFTER A GLIDE THROUGH ENGLISH BAY OFF VANCOUVER'S KITSILANO BEACH PARK.

OPPOSITE:
IS THE FISHERMAN HOPING FOR A LATE CATCH ON VANCOUVER'S ENGLISH BAY AWARE OF THE NEONLIKE COLORS SURROUNDING HIM? OR IS HIS VISION RESTRICTED TO THE POTENTIAL FOR A SEAFOOD DINNER?

OVERLEAF:
VOLLEYBALLERS DON'T KNOW WHEN TO QUIT AT KITSILANO BEACH, BESIDE VANCOUVER'S ENGLISH BAY.

NATURAL SELECTION

Jim Sutherland

Here is a revelation: The environment is under stress, and conflict often results when competing interests offer differing solutions.

Here in "Ecotopia," as California writer Ernest Callenbach called this region in his 1975 novel of the same name, we certainly have heard that before. Far from a passing fad among some extremists, since the 1960s, ecological awareness and activism have gone mainstream here. Pacific Northwesterners are in tune with and devoted to their natural surroundings in a manner that's extraordinary in the capitalistic Western Hemisphere. Unfortunately, our high environmental passions sometimes divide us as much as they might connect us.

At a local cocktail party, the polite individual will exhaust the topics of sex, politics, and religion before uttering the words "spotted owl" or "clear-cut." Meanwhile, the entire state of Washington has a running feud with Victoria, British Columbia, because that city persists in flowing its untreated sewage down a pipe into the Strait of Juan de Fuca. And though locals are often entertained by the energetic competition between Seattle and Vancouver, both of which strive to be known as the fastest-growing city on the continent, the reasons for their expansion and the effects it could have on the region disturb many people—not all of them slow-growthers or no-growthers. As usual, jobs draw people here. But conditions elsewhere are also pushing people out of wherever they were before. Many people used to wind up at Vancouver and Seattle in flight from personal problems, whether it was poverty, unemployment, or, entirely too frequently, the law. Now, many of them are driven here by public troubles. Ask the Angelenos pouring into Seattle or the Torontonians and Hong Kongers swelling Vancouver why they've come, and they'll mention fires, earthquakes, escalating crime rates, bad air and water, and overcrowding elsewhere. It's as if Malthus himself were speaking.

So why did so many of these affluent pilgrims choose Washington and British Columbia as their destinations? The answer is obvious. Looking west from Seattle and north or west from Vancouver, the view, after all, is of mountains, ocean, forest, and what many find a quite startling absence of human activity.

Some consider the mountains enough of an attraction. Both cities boast snow-covered volcanic peaks within easy gaze—Rainier from Seattle, Baker from Vancouver—which are scarcely less impressive than Japan's iconic Mount Fuji. (It also used to be possible to stand at the top of Seattle's Space Needle and glimpse grand Mount Saint Helens, but then the peak blew itself spectacularly to bits in a 1980 eruption.) Vancouverites are especially fortunate; their North Shore mountains rise directly out of the city's eastern and northern suburbs. So rugged are those peaks, and so untraveled, that it is possible to step off a cul-de-sac, walk northward for five days, and emerge after an arduous journey on a similar cul-de-sac in a small town fifty miles away without ever seeing another person. More practically, it is possible to spend a pleasant afternoon climbing to the top of any of several suburban mile-high mountains. On one of them, Grouse, you can even enjoy a meal and a drink before taking the lift down.

Then there is the ocean. Thoroughly sheltered in both cities, it serves as a playground for two of the world's great pleasure boat armadas. However, it's still pristine enough to provide regular sightings of perhaps the most spectacular marine animal of them all, the orca or killer whale.

The ocean, in conjunction with the winds, is responsible for the Northwest's shockingly temperate climate. Think about this: Vancouver lies on about the same latitude as southern Labrador or Irkutsk, in Russian Siberia. Yet winter temperatures are mild enough that certain types of palm trees thrive, and one ambitious Vancouver homeowner has coaxed a front yard full of subtropical trees to heights of up to twenty feet. The explanation resides in southwesterlies so prevailing that by the time they reach the continent, they have attained roughly the same temperature as the warm ocean they've been passing over for days. (On a sometimes less appreciated note, those winds spent the same number of days sucking up ocean water, which they then dump on the land.) Only during summer and fall do the westerlies die down and even reverse, providing a generous window of weather that is pleasingly dry and generally warm, though almost never hot.

It is this mild and wet regime, of course, that makes possible the third and perhaps most important element in the region's potent ecosystem: the forests. Lots of places, after all, front the ocean, and more than a few have mountains of their own. But there is quite literally nothing on the globe to rival the Pacific Coast rain forests.

By any measure, the redwoods, Douglas firs, Sitka spruce, western hemlocks, and western red cedars that stretch in various combinations from northern California to the Alaskan Panhandle are the biggest trees on earth. Several top out in the range of three hundred feet—as tall as a thirty-story building. Many trunks measure twenty feet across, the size of a small house. A mere acre of old-growth forest can support a biomass approaching one thousand tons of living material, the weight of fifteen thousand people. These trees can live considerably more than a millennium and, after they die, spend most of the next thousand years decomposing. Early in the twentieth century, a Seattle civic official had a four-hundred-foot Douglas fir that stood in a city park chopped down for firewood, which he sold for personal gain. Today, such a tree would yield wood worth some fifty thousand dollars.

Yet there is much more to Northwest forests than mere numbers. To understand their appeal, a person need only spend a few minutes in the old-growth forest that once covered this region. There isn't much left, especially not in easily accessible areas, but remnants are preserved in Vancouver's Stanley Park and in West Seattle's Schmitz Park. Words fail miserably in describing the truly sublime moss- and fern-draped scene.

It is perhaps not surprising that the preservation of these forests became *the* environmental issue of the 1990s, not just locally but across much of the world. What is surprising is that it didn't happen earlier. In 1971, when the environmental watchdog group Greenpeace was formed in Vancouver, its object of protest had nothing to do with forests (the family of one of the founders, after all, ran a logging company) but, rather, with nuclear weapons testing and then whale hunting. When, around the same time, a young Oregon researcher determined that the northern spotted owl required large tracts of old-growth forest to survive, environmentalists failed to realize that the owl's imminent extinction gave them a handy weapon to use in trying to preserve remaining ancient forests. In fact, given the value of logging and the region's traditional resource-extraction economy, few thought that such a goal was possible, or even particularly desirable.

By the early 1980s, though, the clear-cutting of successive pristine watersheds was becoming an issue in British Columbia. As the idea percolated, the conflict grew, culminating in the 1990s in the massive Clayoquot Sound confrontation, European boycotts of B.C. forest products, and the province's international censure as the "Brazil of the North." Awareness eventually led to action. As of mid-decade, vast areas of British Columbia once destined for logging had been set aside as parks, and the practice of clear-cutting was on its way out. In the United States, meanwhile, the spotted owl controversy had resulted in the cessation of logging across much of the remaining old-growth forest. To the surprise of almost everyone, the preservationists had won a qualified victory.

Everyone, that is, except the New Ecotopians, those hundreds of thousands of people who, over the last few years, have increased the population of Seattle and Vancouver.

These people, it should be pointed out, are not the same ones Callenbach envisioned when he coined the term Ecotopia. In his optimistic 1975 novel, America's Pacific Northwest had become a pollution-free land where the internal combustion engine was outlawed, working hours were restricted to twenty a week, and sexual promiscuity was officially sanctioned during annual holidays accompanying the solstices and equinoxes (Callenbach was writing, of course, before the advent of the AIDS epidemic). Nor are they the same ones Joel Garreau knew six years later, when he popularized the term Ecotopia with his influential book *The Nine Nations of North America*. Garreau anticipated the declining importance of international borders by extending Ecotopia up the coast into British Columbia, but he persisted in seeing the region as something of a hippie haven.

Most modern Northwesterners wouldn't know patchouli to smell it. But they have seen idealistic, if feckless, communism fall, sensible but uncaring capitalism triumph, and the dawning Information Revolution threaten to wreak as much social havoc in the twenty-first century as the Industrial Revolution did in the nineteenth. They know where they want to spend the next few decades of change, and it's the same sort of place that a lot of other smart people are starting to crave: a pleasantly isolated region rich with food, water, and plenty of natural resources, where they can find a good job and a nice life.

That's why, although compromises will be made and growing cities will sprawl alarmingly, the dominant ethic of this region will continue to revolve around environmentalism. The New Ecotopians have seen the rest of the world. In fact, they help run it. And now that they've moved to the suburbs—Cascadia, that is—they'll do whatever has to be done to keep its troubles away from their neighborhood.

AT THE BASE OF 170-FOOT NOOKSACK FALLS, IN THE SNOQUALMIE NATIONAL FOREST NORTHEAST OF SEATTLE, THE VIOLENT RUSH OF WATER QUIETS TO A SIBILANT STREAM.

PAST IMPERFECT

J. Kingston Pierce

Other western towns experienced their defining boom times deep into the nineteenth century or early in the twentieth. Think of San Francisco or the Yukon's Dawson City, both of which were transformed into minor metropolises almost overnight by this continent's two richest gold rushes. Or consider Dallas, which was little more than a raw spot beside Texas's Trinity River until the 1920s, when it suddenly discovered itself surrounded by five major oil-producing tracts.

Seattle and Vancouver watched enviously as those other places rolled giddily in the clover of their own good fortune. It was a cruel joke on Victorian immigrants to Gastown, the civic seed from which Vancouver grew, that the Native Americans who had lived there previously called their home *Luck-Lucky* (meaning "grove of beautiful trees"): Luck was in short supply during the burg's early days as filth, financial failure, and fire made a mockery of its founders' dreams. The first white families in the Seattle area at least showed a modicum of humor about how difficult it would be to carve any satellite of civilization out of this darkly forested realm. They dubbed their initial colony New York-*Alki*, translated from the Northwest Coast Chinook jargon as "New York By-and-By."

It was predicted, from their inceptions, that these two frontier outposts would fail. Completely. Miserably. The nearby settlements that demonstrated far better abilities to capture public attention and private dollars appeared more likely to thrive. In their first half century, every time Vancouver or Seattle enjoyed a boom, it seemed soon to be followed by a bust. Critics joked that the only reason these municipalities didn't collapse was that residents failed to understand just how dramatically the odds were stacked against them.

So you can understand why people living in today's twin capitals of Cascadia might sound a tad skeptical about their latest local swells of prosperity—surges fed by Pacific Rim commerce, fattened by influxes of computer whizzes and aspiring artists, and fawned over by the media. After all, San Francisco and Dawson City both thought their booms ensured great things ahead. Only one of them was right.

It was the present, however, not yet the future that concerned the two-dozen-odd adults and children who debarked from the schooner *Exact* at Alki Point, just west of modern-day Seattle, on November 13, 1851. Led by Midwesterners Arthur and David Denny, Carson Boren, and William Bell, the party had spent months traveling cross-country, enduring malarial fevers and assaults on their food by skunks, only to arrive at their promised land in a torrential downpour.

"I remember it rained awful hard that day—and the starch got took out of our bonnets and the wind blew," wrote the wife of *Exact* Captain Robert Fay, who was along for the ride, "and when the women got into the rowboat to go ashore they were crying every one of 'em…and the last glimpse I had of them was the women standing under the trees with their wet sun bonnets all lopping down over their faces and their aprons to their eyes."

An inauspicious beginning, to be sure. And things got worse. It took but a short while for the tiny band to realize that although New York-Alki offered spectacular panoramas of Puget Sound and the spiny-backed Olympic Mountains, its shallow, windy harbor and distant tree line made it an imperfect anchorage for ships loading the site's single marketable resource: timber, much in demand in burgeoning San Francisco.

Within three months, the young pioneers abandoned their original landing and moved east across deep Elliott Bay to a hilly, well-treed claim on its far side, where a Duwamish Indian village had stood. Goaded on by a personable but unsuccessful merchant from the Midwest, Dr. David Swinton Maynard, who was determined to make his interests on the Sound pay off, they surveyed city blocks, reared homes, and—most important—erected a steam-powered sawmill that would draw trading vessels to their corner of Puget Sound. This last was the enterprise of a laconic Ohioan, Henry Yesler, who had planned his mill for Alki but was convinced by the Boren-Maynard group to build on Elliott Bay instead. As an incentive, they gave Yesler not only 320 acres of old-growth forest above the town but also a ribbon of property linking it to the water-front, down which oxen could drag evergreens for milling. That strip—layered at one time with small, greased logs—was known for years as Mill Street and is now Yesler Way, but early on it earned the sobriquet by which it has become famous: Skid Road.

Once it looked as if they might not be washed away by rains after all, or impoverished for lack of outside trade, the handful of movers and shakers at Elliott Bay were anxious to designate their hamlet in some distinctive manner. So, to honor an elderly leader of the Suquamish natives, they called it Sealth—or, as white tongues found it easier to pronounce, "Seattle."

Unfortunately, this tribute neither pleased nor appeased Chief Sealth's people. Apparently, they were superstitious about their names being used during their lifetimes.

It further strained race relations to have squatters encroaching, with increasing audacity, on hard-won Indian treaty lands. Sealth managed to keep his followers peaceful, but chiefs living east of the Cascade Range were less forbearing. In late 1855, families in the White River Valley (immediately north of the present city of Auburn) were slain by native raiders. On January 25, 1856, the violence reached Seattle. As many as three hundred armed Indians, led by Yakamas and Nisquallies, descended upon the community, chasing residents to a log blockhouse at the foot of Cherry Street and drawing cannon fire from the United States warship *Decatur*, which had come to defend American settlers.

This attack preceded two more months of sporadic fighting nearby (and another couple of years of clashes across Washington Territory). Many homes were reduced to ashes. Maybe a dozen whites and scores of Indians lost their lives. Elliott Bay's aborning society fell into a decade-long slump. The saddest result of the hostilities, however, was that they broke the bonds of trust between early Seattleites and their indigenous neighbors. Even today, Native Americans on Puget Sound haven't fully recovered from the racial oppression that followed the "Battle of Seattle."

Captain George Vancouver, who explored Puget Sound in 1792 aboard the English sloop-of-war *Discovery*, had, through his published writings, led the Dennys, Borens, and many others before them to believe that establishing a modern habitation in the Pacific Northwest would be much easier than it was. But then, he'd never actually tried to do it.

Dispatched into this remote territory to assert Britain's interests here and search one last time for the fabled Northwest Passage—a navigable transcontinental water-way—Vancouver's principal task was to observe and report back to King George III, which he did in rhapsodic detail. "To describe the beauties of this region will on some future occasion be a very grateful task to the pen of a skillful panegyrist," Vancouver remarked. "The serenity of the climate, the innumerable pleasing landscapes, and the abundant fertility that unassisted nature puts forth, require only to be enriched by the industry of men with villages, mansions, cottages, and other buildings, to render it the most lovely country that can be imagined...."

The sullen thirty-five-year-old captain spent months among Cascadia's isles and inlets. With the *Discovery* and its smaller consort, the *Chatham*, he reconnoitered the Sound and then sailed north across today's United States–Canada border to inspect English Bay and the Stanley Park peninsula. Along the way, his crew parleyed with native peoples, the vast majority of whom—whether they were Nisqually, Skagit, or Musqueam—lived in plank homes and compact groups, relished a bounty of seafoods, and demonstrated fine woodworking skills (though not usually in the form of totem poles, which were carved primarily by Indians farther up the British Columbia coast).

Musing upon the Northwest's eventual value, one of Vancouver's subalterns, Joseph Whidbey, fancied it would make an ideal dump for convicts released from Australian prison colonies, "lest they return to England to become a fresh Prey upon the Public." Fortunately, his mapmaking commander had bigger expectations in mind, which explains why so many landmarks here recall people George Vancouver respected: Mount Rainier, Port Townsend, Burrard Inlet, and, most meaningful, Puget Sound, which exalts his second lieutenant, Peter Puget, the man who scouted out the southern extremities of Cascadia's inland sea.

Other adventurers—Russian, Spanish, and English—had preceded Captain Vancouver to these parts, and more would follow. In 1808, for instance, Simon Fraser, a partner with the North West Company, a Montreal-based fur-trading concern then in competition with the larger Hudson's Bay Company (HBC), canoed the British Columbia waterway that now bears his name, believing—mistakenly—that it would lead him south all the way to the Columbia River. The United States government's first oceangoing expedition to this sector arrived in 1841, led by Lieutenant Charles Wilkes. Like Vancouver, Wilkes was awed by the environment. "I venture nothing in saying, there is no country in the world that possesses waters equal to these," he wrote. In fact, so glowing was the lieutenant's account that it stiffened the United States President James K. Polk's resolve to draw the American–Canadian border east from the lower tip of Russian Alaska, rather than from the mouth of the Columbia, as Britain proposed. A compromise in 1846 finally limited the Crown's hegemony to lands north of the 49th parallel, as well as Vancouver Island. (Even then, tensions didn't end completely. The so-called Pig War of 1859, sparked by the shooting of a British hog that had wandered into an American potato patch in the San Juan Islands, at the north end of Puget Sound, provoked a thirteen-year dispute over control of the straits of Juan de Fuca and Georgia.)

Yet none of those subsequent explorations overshadowed George Vancouver's. Is it any wonder, then, that his moniker should have been borrowed by British Columbia's foremost city?

Of course, anybody who lived before the 1880s in what is now Greater Vancouver would have been hard-pressed to argue that their settlement *deserved* association with the renowned navigator.

Perhaps twenty thousand Native Americans trod the shores of Burrard Inlet when white mountain men and assorted outlaws—"the very scum of the earth," as one HBC official phrased it—began showing up there in the 1820s to trap beaver for profit. Gold strikes in 1858 along the Fraser River and in the Cariboo Mountains of central British Columbia brought another breed of rabble to the area: twenty-five thousand prospectors. Few of these men so much as passed within sight of Burrard Inlet, but they affected its development, nonetheless. In 1858, London's Parliament, concerned that this new domain needed the bridle of law and eager to tax the flood of miners, created the Crown colony of British Columbia, putting James Douglas, already the governor of Vancouver Island, in charge of the entire province. He, in turn, set up his new government—not at Victoria, as many had anticipated (since that island town was the colony's largest), but at New Westminster, a nascent port on the Fraser River that Douglas strengthened in order to discourage armed American incursions over the border. This power shift ultimately attracted new pioneers and income to all of British Columbia's lower mainland.

The present-day site of Vancouver didn't enjoy its first significant attentions, though, until after the gold had petered out and financial depression was setting in.

In 1862, as the American Civil War raged at the other end of the continent, a troika of Brits bought acreage between Coal Harbour and English Bay (in today's chic West End) and announced plans to start a brick-making business. This proposal, in a spot where timber was a cheap and plentiful building material, struck the locals as barmy, and they soon labeled the partners the "Three Greenhorns." Over the next decade, however, as sawmills sprang up on both sides of Burrard Inlet and their lumber was exported to South America and across the Pacific (flawless beams were even sent from British Columbia to help build the Imperial Palace in Peking), business entrepreneurs conceded there might indeed be some potential here.

One of the first to capitalize on it was John "Gassy Jack" Deighton. Garrulous and bearded, a retired riverboat pilot and onetime gold seeker, Deighton arrived at Burrard Inlet in 1867. As soon as he got thirsty, he realized that while there were ample mills around with plenty of workers, the closest saloon was in New Westminster—*half a day's walk away.* So he decided to open a more convenient groggery and hotel on the inlet's southern shore (at the present intersection of Water and Carrall streets). Around this quickly gathered a tiny, chaotic village known, after its unlikely first citizen, as Gastown. It wasn't much; one mill operator described it as an "aggregation of filth." The local economy yo-yoed with fluctuations in the international lumber market, the surrounding land proved unfit for farming, and the population was so heterogeneous (Indians mixing with whites of every nationality) that all daily interaction—from commerce to court cases—could be conducted in nothing better than pidgin Chinook. Whatever meager prestige Gastown had realized through its proximity to British Columbia's capital vanished in 1868, as the government decamped finally to Victoria.

Two years later, when Deighton's settlement was properly incorporated under the name Granville, it seemed a hopelessly optimistic gesture. British Columbia had recently joined the Canadian Confederation and was soon to be tied to the rest of the dominion via the Canadian Pacific Railway (CPR). But the train's westernmost terminus was expected to be New Westminster or Port Moody, at the eastern extreme of Burrard Inlet, or maybe Victoria (by way of a bridge spanning Queen Charlotte Strait). In any case, Gastown/Granville gave every indication of remaining a backwater.

Then William Cornelius Van Horne changed everything. As general manager of the Canadian Pacific Railroad, it was up to him to select the new terminus, and in 1884 he gave the surprising nod to Granville. He'd been impressed by the town's early strivings toward civilization (in 1882, it installed the first electric lighting north of San Francisco) as well as by its deepwater port—the jumping-off point, Van Horne imagined, for ships connecting the Far East with his transcontinental rail line. Integral to this deal was that the provincial government deed the CPR 6,000 acres (2,430 hectares) of property adjacent to the town—which it did—and work commenced promptly on new streets and blocks. (That CPR grant, by the way, included all of what today constitutes the core of Vancouver.) In addition, the general manager claimed the right to re-christen the town once again, to give it a handle that would resonate with influential CPR investors in England. "This eventually is destined to be a great city in Canada," Van Horne supposedly told his chief surveyor. "We must see that it has a name that will designate its place on the map….Vancouver it shall be…."

No matter that there already existed a much older city of Vancouver, founded in 1825 on the north shoulder of the Columbia River, in what would become Washington State; Granville formally adopted the name on April 6, 1886. Between February and May of that year, seven hundred new buildings were raised, bringing the total to roughly one thousand. The town's 125 citizens elected a mayor and aldermen. And they initiated plans to convert a federal military reserve into Stanley Park—a 1,000-acre (405-hectare) greensward, named for Lord Stanley, a Canadian governor-general, that in the 1880s was considered so far to the west of town that many folks complained it would never be used. Vancouver was showing signs of being Luck-Lucky after all.

Even the fire of June 13, 1886, ignited by brush burners clearing land and spread by fickle winds, barely slowed vicinal growth. With no fire-fighting equipment available, the wooden town was reduced to a mephitic smudge in less than an hour. At least twenty people died. Yet within a week, sanguine businessmen were reestablishing themselves in tents, and in under six months, visitors to Vancouver found a skyline of brick and stone buildings that challenged the height of Douglas fir trees. When the first cross-country train arrived on May 23, 1887—the eve of Queen Victoria's sixty-eighth birthday—Van Horne's prophecy of a great city beside Burrard Inlet seemed at last to be coming true.

Seattle, by this time, had spent fifteen years unsuccessfully lobbying for its own major

rail link. The closest it had come was in 1872, three years after its official incorporation, when the Northern Pacific Railroad appeared interested. Alas, when NP directors announced the pot at the end of their new steel rainbow, it was Tacoma, a younger and rival town, located about thirty-five miles south on Puget Sound. (Henry Villard, president of the Northern Pacific, did lay a spur line in 1883, connecting Seattle with Tacoma and Portland, Oregon, but it only operated for a short time and reinforced the city's second-class status.)

Many of the people who had moved to Elliott Bay in anticipation of the NP project and the jobs it would create had left by 1880. Those who stayed often found employment difficult to find. By mid-decade, white laborers had focused the blame for their continuing idleness on Chinese immigrants, a good share of whom had worked for low wages on the transcontinental railroad to California and then, when that was finished in 1869, drifted north to find other jobs—or *steal* jobs, as white provocateurs contended. In February 1886, mobs of Sinophobes invaded Seattle's Chinatown and herded almost all of its 350 to 400 occupants toward steamships bound for San Francisco. Martial law was declared to halt the expulsion, but at least half of the Chinese wound up leaving anyway, fearful of the consequences should they stay. (A year later, Vancouver weathered the first of its own anti-Chinese uprisings. A second and more serious one occurred in 1907.)

Amazingly, through all of this, Seattle retained an "exceptional public spirit," as one visitor of the times described it. Gone was the railroad, yet the city had a

COMMERCIAL LOGGING IN THE PACIFIC NORTHWEST BEGAN IN 1788, WHEN CAPTAIN JOHN MEARES, A RETIRED LIEUTENANT OF THE BRITISH ROYAL NAVY, ARRIVED IN BRITISH COLUMBIA WITH MEN READY TO FELL TREES AND SHAPE THEM INTO SPARS AND TIMBER THAT COULD BE SOLD TO SHIPBUILDERS IN CHINA. AWED BY THE ABUNDANCE OF TREES HERE, MEARES WROTE THAT "THE WOODS OF THIS PART OF AMERICA ARE CAPABLE OF SUPPLYING WITH THEIR VALUABLE MATERIALS, ALL THE NAVIES OF EUROPE." CASCADIA FORESTS HAVE RARELY BEEN STILL SINCE.

LEFT:
INCREASING INTERNATIONAL DEMAND FOR CASCADIAN TIMBER DROVE LOGGERS TO PUSH DEEPER AND DEEPER INTO FORESTS, LOOKING FOR THE HIGHEST-QUALITY TREES. BY THE 1920S, BRITISH COLUMBIA'S MERRILL & RING LUMBER COMPANY AND ITS COMPETITORS HAD LAID TRAIN TRACKS INTO STANDS OF OLD-GROWTH, HOPING TO MOVE THOSE NATURAL RESOURCES MORE QUICKLY TO MARKET. COURTESY VANCOUVER PUBLIC LIBRARY, PHOTO NO. 1521

Territorial University (the future University of Washington, founded in 1861) and was building up trade with Alaska. Grand hotels dotted the hills, schools were opening, and an iron-and-steel works had been planned for the east side of Lake Washington (an enterprise that never got off the ground, though it did spawn the suburb of Kirkland).

Local resilience reached its height on June 6, 1889, when Seattle's original downtown—today's Pioneer Square historic district—began to burn. Almost exactly three years after Vancouver's big blaze, a pot of glue boiled over a gasoline stove and into a mess of turpentine-soaked wood shavings left on the floor of a woodworker's basement. Within half an hour, entire city blocks had been consumed by fire, and hydrant pressure was too low to adequately combat the calamity's progress. Flames licked ravenously at wooden storefronts and chased horses into madness down cluttered alleyways. While church bells clamored and dynamite widened fire breaks, men and boys pulled hose carts and the town's first steam-powered fire engine through dusty, rutted streets. They dodged mothers towing their children; prisoners shackled together in flight from the old courthouse; and half-clad prostitutes fleeing the red-light district mere steps ahead of their clients—sachems whose characteristic dignity was undermined by the fact that they were still hiking up their pants.

Seattle's Great Fire of 1889 lasted twelve and a half hours. By the time its fury was spent, thirty central-city blocks—a total of sixty-four acres (twenty-six hectares)—had been leveled.

However, not a single human life is known to have been lost in the disaster. And that may be why businessmen and politicians barely caught their breaths before starting to rebuild. There was little to mourn except the passing of an often troubled era that most people didn't mind forgetting. Seattle wanted to reinvent itself. It was

EXTRAORDINARILY TALL TREES WERE CUT UP IN SECTIONS, MAKING THE WORK EASIER AND SOMEWHAT LESS DANGEROUS. BUT LOGGING HAS ALWAYS BEEN A RISKY BUSINESS. IN HIS BOOK *HOLY OLD MACKINAW,* HISTORIAN STEWART HOLBROOK RECALLED WHAT IT WAS LIKE WORKING IN A FOREST AMONG FALLING TREES: "WHEN THE GIANT GIVES ITS FIRST SLIGHT SHUDDER OF DEATH, THE FALLER SOUNDS THE LOGGER'S TRADITIONAL WARNING CRY OF 'TIM-BERRRRR!,' A WAIL WITH A RISING INFLECTION—OFTEN THE LAST HUMAN SOUND HEARD BY HEEDLESS MEN." COURTESY VANCOUVER PUBLIC LIBRARY, PHOTO NO. 1582

encouraged by Elmer H. Fisher, an energetically self-promoting architect from Scotland who snapped up most of the prime building commissions available after the fire. Fisher established the Richardsonian Romanesque design vernacular still so familiar in Pioneer Square, especially in his own stone-and-brick Pioneer Building, at First Avenue and Yesler Way. Engineers and reformers picked up where Fisher left off, raising streets higher above the waterline, regrading Seattle's steep topography to ease horse and streetcar travel, and trying to purge the twin terrors of villainy and vice from their business district. When, six months after the fire, Washington earned its statehood, Seattleites were more than ready for a celebration.

Four years later, the city's biggest dream at last came true: James J. Hill's Great Northern Railroad opened easy access between Elliott Bay and the East. Too bad its inauguration came just in time to carry job seekers out of Seattle, at least those who hadn't already killed themselves as a result of the Panic of 1893—not the nation's first depression, but its worst yet.

Brought on by softness in European markets, inflated silver prices that reduced the United States government's gold reserves, and a Republican-controlled Congress that had profligately spent away $100 million in Treasury surplus funds, the panic thundered west from Wall Street. In Seattle, as elsewhere, a run on banks ensued, depositors withdrawing their savings and converting them to gold whenever possible. Land values sank by as much as 80 percent. Within a year, eleven local banks had bolted their doors. Overextended nabobs had to borrow from the only person in town whose business seemed unaffected by the downturn: Lou Graham, the owner of a most orderly disorderly house, who would lend them money for political leverage down the road.

Having become dependent on international shipping, Vancouver was also hard hit by this depression. The CPR's transcontinental trade kept some money coming in, but it was more than offset by farm-flooding losses in the Fraser Valley.

No less jolting than the depression itself was the event that wrenched Seattle and Vancouver back up from their doldrums: the Klondike Gold Rush.

In 1896, word of major nugget finds along a tributary of the Klondike River, in Canada's Yukon Territory, began filtering down. Then in mid-July of 1897, a steamer nosed into the San Francisco docks with a million dollars' worth of treasure out of the north. This was followed, on July 17, by the passenger ship *Portland*'s much heralded arrival at Elliott Bay. It carried almost two tons of gold, plus sixty-eight "sourdoughs" sharing incredible tales of the easy fortunes to be found in the Yukon.

Newspapers spread the word: GOLD IN THE KLONDIKE! And though hardly anyone knew precisely where the Klondike was, they all suddenly wanted to go there. Crews operating the ferries between Vancouver and Victoria abandoned their jobs and headed toward Skagway, Alaska, the main off-loading point for miners headed to the goldfields around Dawson City. They were followed by cops, newspapermen, and preachers from all over the Northwest. The mayor of Seattle, W. D. Wood, didn't even bother to come home; he telegraphed his resignation from San Francisco, raised money to buy a ship, and was so excited about sailing north that he forgot to load fifty thousand pounds of his passengers' belongings and was almost lynched at dockside.

TIMBER BARON AND
ENGINEER WILLIAM
BOEING'S FASCINATION
WITH FLYING BEGAN
WHEN HE ATTENDED A
CALIFORNIA AIR MEET IN
1910. FIVE YEARS
LATER, HE BOUGHT HIS
FIRST AIRCRAFT, A
FLOATPLANE, BUT
QUICKLY DAMAGED ITS
PONTOONS WHEN HE
TRIED TO LAND ON
PUGET SOUND.
REALIZING THAT THERE
WAS NO LOCAL SOURCE
FOR SPARE PARTS, HE
DECIDED TO BUILD HIS
OWN PONTOONS—AND
DESIGN A SUPERIOR
VERSION OF THE PLANE
HIMSELF. THE REST IS
HISTORY.
ABOVE:
BY 1917, HIS NEW
AVIATION ENTERPRISE
HAD ESTABLISHED
ITSELF ON THE
DUWAMISH RIVER, IN
THE STORIED "RED
BARN," WHICH BOEING
HAD INTENDED AS THE
PLACE WHERE HIS YACHT
MIGHT BE BUILT. IT WAS
THERE THAT MANY
PLANES WERE BUILT FOR
MILITARY USE DURING
WORLD WAR I.
(THE RED BARN IS NOW
PART OF SEATTLE'S
MUSEUM OF FLIGHT.)
COURTESY THE BOEING
COMPANY ARCHIVES
BELOW:
THE END OF THE WAR
CAUSED THE COMPANY'S
FIRST DECLINE, AS
AIRCRAFT ORDERS
FELL OFF, AND
BOEING TURNED TO
MANUFACTURING
SPEEDBOATS AND
BEDROOM FURNITURE
AND DELIVERING
AIRMAIL. THIS WING,
BEING SEWN OVER WITH
CANVAS IN 1922, MIGHT
HAVE BEEN FITTED ONTO
ONE OF THE COMPANY'S
AIRMAIL BIPLANES.
COURTESY THE BOEING
COMPANY ARCHIVES

Although most of the men (and fewer women) who landed at Dawson City between 1897 and 1900 never found their El Dorados, Vancouver and Seattle both grew rich during the Klondike frenzy, especially the latter city, which promoted itself as the "Gateway to Alaska." Seattle entrepreneurs had gotten busy right away opening mining schools. Hotels sprang up almost overnight to accommodate thousands of transients. Outfitters, capitalizing on a strict Canadian law that required prospectors trekking inland from Skagway to Dawson City to pack along a ton of supplies—enough to live on for a year—found their own bonanza in the five hundred to one thousand dollars that each miner had to fork out for those provisions. Men who still had money in their pockets could lose it at Lou Graham's cathouse or elsewhere in Seattle's red-light district. What were a few dollars, they figured, when unimagined wealth awaited them on the Klondike River?

"Seattle," the *New York Herald* reported in 1898, "has gone stark, staring mad on gold."

Many of those who stopped at Cascadia en route to or from the Klondike never left. They were joined by easterners and European immigrants. By 1900, as the gold rush was winding down, Seattle's population exceeded 80,000, and Vancouver claimed 27,000 residents—in both cases, twice as many people as they'd had only a decade before. Within another ten years, there were 100,000 Vancouverites. Seattle, housing a quarter of a million inhabitants, had surpassed Portland and Tacoma as the American Northwest's largest city.

All of these new people would drive land values up, open or enrich new suburbs in both cities, and create new business opportunities. While Seattle emphasized its talents as a shipbuilder, Vancouver flourished as a center for resource commerce. Lumber was being shipped everywhere. Canned fish went out to the United Kingdom and Australia. Mining speculation in western Canada led to the establishment of the Vancouver Stock Exchange (VSE) in 1907—an enterprise that then, as now, raised eyebrows. (One editorial of the time called the VSE's dozen organizers "sharpies with gilt-edged tongues and junk securities.")

Prosperity also allowed Vancouver and Seattle to cultivate an air of refinement. Residents of Burrard Inlet promoted the arts, made an elite address out of the West End, and improved the leisure amenities around Stanley Park. Meanwhile, on Elliott Bay, burghers in 1903 hired the scions of famed landscape architect Frederick Law Olmsted to develop for their city a twenty-mile belt of new parklands and boulevards that would, as John C. Olmsted envisioned it, "make Seattle known all over the world." With that in progress, the Olmsteds set to work on the grounds of the Alaska-Yukon-Pacific Exposition—Seattle's first world's fair and its official "coming out party," a brilliant confection of terra-cotta and fountains that was held in 1909 on the University of Washington grounds, north of downtown.

But the residents of these two cities did not have long to rest on their laurels. Within a few years, World War I began, drawing more men from Vancouver than from any other city in North America. Three months after Armistice Day, highly unionized Seattle became the setting for the United States' first general labor strike. Then came Prohibition, America's brief campaign to legislate vice out of existence. The idea precipitated some spectacular nighttime raids, as Seattle rumrunners, including former cop Roy Olmstead, tried to smuggle liquor across the British

Columbia border. It boosted the political profile of reform-minded women in Washington State, which led in 1926 to Seattle's election of Bertha Knight Landes as the first woman mayor of a major American city. But Prohibition had little permanent effect on Cascadian drinking habits. It was repealed—with glee—in 1933.

Just when people were starting to enjoy themselves again, the Great Depression closed businesses and stopped construction everywhere, except for the shantytowns to which men with no work and less hope drifted. In Vancouver, schools and fish canneries closed, and riots erupted as men disgusted with low wages at government work camps demanded an economic turnaround. In Seattle, the destitute huddled along Yesler Way, the cant name for which had been mangled as "Skid Row," a term that spread to other down-at-heels districts around the continent.

World War II snapped the region out of its malaise, creating a demand for Boeing aircraft and naval ships from the yards at Vancouver, Victoria, and Bremerton, just across Puget Sound from Seattle. Tens of thousands of people arrived in this region to answer want ads. They were often met on the assembly lines by women taking advantage of the war to escape their kitchens in pursuit of paying work. The only people not welcome in employment lines, it appeared, were the Japanese. Deemed a security risk—despite the fact that many of them had been born in North America—they were sent to United States and Canadian internment camps by the thousands, to be released en masse only toward the end of the war. By then, a new and different round of racial problem emerged in Seattle, as African-Americans, who had been invited to take wartime industrial jobs, found themselves unwelcome and unemployed after the fighting ended. By the 1960s, they were ready to rebel in Seattle, as elsewhere across the United States.

Looking back, it's easy to diminish the importance of these episodes and later ones in Cascadian history. To think, for instance, that the 1962 Century 21 Exposition—Seattle's second major fair, the one that gave us both an Elvis Presley film *(It Happened at the World's Fair)* and the bizarre Space Needle—was quaint and merely distracting rather than seminal. We may pass off Vancouver's successful fight against a city-splitting freeway as a lesser victory than it seemed in the 1970s. Or we could recall how depressed Seattleites were in 1970 and 1971, when Boeing laid off sixty thousand people—two-thirds of its work force—but now only laugh at the bumper stickers that read "Will the last person to leave Seattle please turn out the lights?" For some people, it might even be possible to forget Seattle's Green River Killer, still at large after about fifty murders, or Ted Bundy, the Seattle attorney and Republican campaigner who murdered between three dozen and one hundred women before his Florida electrocution in 1989. When we read stories from the 1980s and 1990s that questioned the changes to be wrought on Vancouver by thousands of immigrating Hong Kongers, will we think one day, Why did they worry so much?

A century from now, Cascadians will be wondering at our own era. Will they chide or applaud us for our ultra-chic glass towers, our efforts to preserve Vancouver's Gastown and Seattle's Pike Place Market, our coffee craze, "Generation X" authors, and clawings after international notoriety? Will they shake their heads at our fragile belief that today's boom years will last forever? Or will they shake their heads and ask, "Why did they worry so much?"

Cities at the End of the Rainbow

David M. Buerge

Look in a hotel drawer in downtown Vancouver and you will find a copy of *The Teachings of the Buddha* alongside the Gideon Bible. In Seattle, shellfish harvesting regulations are posted on city beaches in Vietnamese and Cambodian as well as English. Both towns have turbaned Sikhs driving taxicabs, and their stores advertise wares in a dozen exotic scripts. Here, at the gateway to the Orient, Asia has hurried through the door.

Seattle and Vancouver are not especially big urban centers, but they have grown quickly and now enjoy reputations as places to be. "There is a tradition," writes British Columbia author Gary Geddes, "that when the good people of Toronto die, they go to Vancouver." Not everyone, though, is thrilled with glowing reports about these spots, for they know how eager outsiders can be to escape busier or more crowded or less vibrant locales and move to Cascadia. After *Harper's* magazine judged Seattle to be America's most livable city, *Seattle Times* columnist Emmett Watson expressed the discomfort many residents feel toward such honors: "I don't want a lot of people coming in and spoiling the place," he groused, "so I tell them it rains here all the time."

Pride of place and ambivalence over newcomers have marked the histories of these two cities since their beginnings. While both are predominantly white and middle class in makeup today, this was not always so, and it may well change again in the future.

Actually, both communities are much older than they claim. Seattle dates its founding to 1851, when twenty-six men, women, and children arrived intent on building a town. The first white person to settle in what is now Vancouver did so in 1862, though the town itself was not incorporated until 1886. Yet ancestors of the Duwamish Indians lived in villages on Seattle's Elliott Bay from at least the sixth century A.D., and the progenitors of Vancouver's First Nations—the Musqueam and the Squamish—had settled near the Fraser River mouth at least three thousand years ago. It is a modern conceit that divides each city's history from the demonstrable existence of these earlier habitations. Clearly, human beings have prized our local real estate for a long, long time.

Native groups began accepting exotic blood here in the late eighteenth century, as non-native traders and explorers arrived. The newcomers were a mixed lot. Vessels bound for the Northwest Coast commonly gained and lost crewmen in ports along the way, and by the time they arrived, their complements included representatives of virtually every race and nationality that happened to be on hand when the tide changed. In 1787, Captain John Meares, landing in British Columbia to cut exportable timber, brought Chinese shipwrights onto the coast, and early accounts mention the odd Spaniard, Scotsman, Japanese, Russian, or Aleut marooned here more or less happily and busily donating genetic material to more or less compliant native women. Trading companies enriched the stew when they manned their posts with Orkneymen, French Canadians, Britons, Americans, and Hawaiians.

One wonders what extraordinary hybrid might have emerged from all this intermingling, but the experiment in multiculturalism was ahead of its time. The California gold rush loosed a flood of eastern immigrants onto the Pacific Coast, and transcontinental railroads accelerated the movement. Seattle started to boom when it received a connection with the Northern Pacific Railroad in 1883, and Vancouver's turn came when the Canadian Pacific's first locomotive pulled into town in 1887.

These burgeoning towns reflected their immigrants' national origins. The people flocking to Seattle, the northernmost of several American cities on the coast, were primarily Yankees out of New England, New York, and the upper Midwest: independent, moralistic egalitarians eager to make money. Because Vancouver became Canada's major mainland Pacific port, people from all the other provinces funneled into its growing neighborhoods, bringing with them a deference to class and a sense of dutiful propriety. One reporter from the London *Times* observed, "Vancouver was never like Seattle. There has been no Pacific Coast Rowdyism, no revolvering, no instance or need of lynch law."

Seattle's European immigrants came primarily from Scandinavia by way of the Great Plains, a hardworking lot with thick accents. European immigrants to Vancouver were predominantly working people from Great Britain, whose presence enhanced the English accent in Canadian life and enriched the new community with Tudor homes, lush gardens, and a devotion to Labour politics. Seattle's Swedes, Norwegians, Danes, and Finns abandoned much of their national identities in the effort to learn a new language, but they still managed to provide locals with a hankering for strong coffee, rich pastry, and abundant grist for the ethnic humor mill. (Question: How do you get a one-armed Swede out of a tree? Answer: Wave.)

The process of assimilation varied in Vancouver and Seattle. However, the presumption of white, middle-class superiority typified both communities. In place of the earlier commerce between races, a system of social, political, and sexual apartheid evolved. Asa Mercer's efforts in the mid-1860s to import East Coast wives for Seattle bachelors brought him fame (and were later immortalized in the television series "Here Comes the Brides"), but he was inspired less by a dearth of local women than by a dearth of *white* women and fear of racial mixing. Despite being named after an Indian chief, Seattle would exile many of its native residents to reservations, and Vancouver's native peoples were not allowed to vote until 1947.

Asian immigrants confronted similar bias. Imported to build railroads, the Chinese sought solace from harsh conditions by living in close neighborhoods inevitably dubbed Chinatowns. Venturesome whites learned to appreciate Cantonese cooking, a welcome and healthy change from greasy down-home vittles. But when booms went bust, white workers accused the lower-paid Chinese of stealing jobs and drove them out of mines and mills to the chant of "the Chinese must go!" Seattle's anti-Chinese riots of 1885–86 were experienced twice in Vancouver. Yet the Chinese did not disappear entirely. Both towns needed willing workers, and Chinese contacts with Asian markets gained increasing value in a world of expanding trade. The same could be said for the Japanese, who arrived in numbers after Chinese expulsions to help fill the labor void.

Integration into Cascadian society was inevitably more difficult for Asian immigrants than for many Europeans. By the time most of the people pouring into North America from southern and eastern Europe reached the West Coast, they had already filtered through eastern cities, spoke a little English, and were familiar enough with national customs to mingle relatively smoothly. Asians, however, hailing from cultures very different from those of Europe and America, had less opportunity to become Westernized before having to make their way in West Coast cities. Mutual incomprehension bred distrust and intolerance.

The makeup of ethnic communities in Seattle and Vancouver mirrored larger national histories. African-Americans fleeing slavery in the South sought greater opportunities in liberal Washington Territory and were among its first settlers. British North America was another goal of many slaves heading north on the "underground railroad," and while few reached distant Seattle and Vancouver, both communities benefited from enterprising individuals such as William Grose, who ran Seattle's first restaurant, and John Sullivan Deas, a South Carolina tinsmith who helped develop Vancouver's first canneries.

Although Canada gained independence in 1867, it remained part of the British Commonwealth, and Vancouver became a destination for black British subjects from the Caribbean and laborers from India. Along with Japanese and Chinese, this latter group became the target of mob violence in 1907, ignited when a spike in Asian immigration to Vancouver coincided with a recession—always a volatile situation. Another tense confrontation unfolded when Vancouver's East Indian community challenged British Columbia's immigration restrictions in 1913: Officials refused to allow 331 Sikh immigrants to disembark from the *Komogata Maru* anchored in Coal Harbour. The influx of Filipino immigrants to the United States after the Philippines became an American colony in 1898 produced similar tensions in the Seattle area.

But prosperity came to those who built bridges rather than walls. In both cities, churches and temples provided places where ethnic identities could be preserved and forums in which individuals from dissimilar cultures could address mutual concerns.

The struggle to create a more inclusive sense of community met with many reverses, the greatest being the forced relocation of thousands of Japanese immigrants and their naturalized descendants following the bombing of Pearl Harbor in 1941. Convinced that these people posed a threat to the security of North America's Pacific coast, government authorities rounded them up in Seattle, Vancouver, and every other West Coast town and sent them off to interior concentration camps.

Ultimately, however, the struggle bore fruit. After World War II, laws segregating African-Americans in the United States were struck down. In Seattle, policies that kept black residents cooped up in a ghetto gradually disappeared, and in Canada, the political isolation of Asian and First Nations peoples ended with the extension of voting rights.

International events continue to alter both cities' ethnic and cultural complexions. The post–World War II influx of Europeans turned Vancouver's Robson Street

ABOVE:
WHEN FIRST ESTABLISHED, STANLEY PARK WAS SO FAR TO THE WEST OF DOWNTOWN VANCOUVER THAT CITY RESIDENTS THOUGHT IT WOULD NEVER BE USED. BUT BY THE 1890S, CARRIAGEWAYS AND PATHS LED MEN IN BOWLERS AND WOMEN WITH PARASOLS INTO THE FORESTED DEPTHS OF WHAT HAD ONCE BEEN A MILITARY RESERVE. VISITORS SEEMED ESPECIALLY FOND OF HAVING THEIR PICTURES TAKEN IN FRONT OF THE LANDMARK HOLLOW TREE. A PHOTOGRAPHER WHO PLIED HIS TRADE BESIDE THE TREE SHOT MANY SCENES OF FAMILIES, BICYCLING BUSINESSMEN, AND PLAYFUL GROUPS OF WOMEN WHO LINKED HANDS AROUND THE 60-FOOT (18-METER) GIRTH OF THIS RED CEDAR.
COURTESY VANCOUVER PUBLIC LIBRARY, PHOTO NO. 17090

BELOW:
NATIVE AMERICANS IN THE VANCOUVER AREA, SUCH AS THESE PHOTOGRAPHED NEAR ALERT BAY IN THE EARLY TWENTIETH CENTURY, ADOPTED EUROPEAN STYLES OF DRESS. BUT THEY DIDN'T SO EASILY ADAPT TO CITY LIVING, MANY CONTINUING TO OCCUPY SHORESIDE TENTS AND TO FISH FROM CANOES. THE TRADITION OF TOTEM CARVING ALSO SURVIVED, EVEN THOUGH THE SYMBOLISM OF PAINTED HEADS AND STYLIZED WOODEN ANIMALS WAS LOST ON THE MAJORITY WHITE POPULATION.
COURTESY VANCOUVER PUBLIC LIBRARY

into "Robsonstrasse," an eclectic thoroughfare of shops and restaurants. Wars in Korea and Southeast Asia led to a surge of peoples from those areas to Seattle's Rainier Valley, an area populated by an earlier generation of Italian-Americans that came to be known as "Garlic Gulch." More recently, turmoil and prosperity in East Asia, Latin America, and the Middle East have produced new streams of immigrants to both cities. The reasons why they come are still the same: the opportunity to start over, to make life better for themselves and their children.

Today, the social fabrics of Cascadia's two principal metropolises boast a vibrant ethnic weave. While Seattle treasures its Yankee values, it also enjoys the powerful beat of the African-American Kwanzaa festival, the rhythmic dance of the Japanese Bon Odori celebration, and bright mariachi music celebrating Mexico's Cinco de Mayo. Vancouver's dedication to civility nurtures the second-largest Chinese community in North America (after San Francisco), street after street of ethnic restaurants, and a thriving Punjabi market near the Sikh temple in a south Vancouver neighborhood. Just as changes in American immigration policy made Seattle a haven for Russian Jews, changes in Canadian law opened doors to immigrants from Hong Kong, China, and Taiwan. While many groups continue to cluster in ethnic neighborhoods—African-Americans in Seattle's Central District, for instance, and Chinese along Vancouver's East Pender Street—old boundaries have begun to blur as newer groups arrive and individuals climb the economic ladder and buy homes in outlying districts.

Problems remain, of course. A Vancouverite tells the story of an East Indian who wanted to take his family to a museum on a family pass. Seeing the group of three generations, the ticket-taker objected: a family pass, he insisted, was meant only for parents and their children. But the man wanted to bring *his* parents, too—they were family, weren't they? In Seattle the abyss yawning between adults from rural Southeast Asia and their children growing up in urban America has contributed to a recent proliferation of violent Asian street gangs.

As government budget cuts imperil Canadian multicultural programs and threaten further reductions in already beleaguered United States social services, private individuals and agencies struggle to keep bridges between disparate groups intact. Given the ambitious nature of their ideals—a democratic, just society—the wonder may not be the problems still looming ahead, but what has already been achieved. One of the more satisfying developments in both cities has been the renewal of interest and respect accorded their original native inhabitants. The effects of a century of apartheid are finally waning. Dramatic examples of Northwest Coast art grace each community, and the Duwamish, Musqueam, Squamish, and neighboring groups are reasserting pride in themselves and their ancient traditions.

In many ways, each of these two towns has embraced the multicultural diversity of their beginnings to become cities of the rainbow. It is not uncommon now to see women in saris and chadors shopping in Seattle malls, and Vancouver television airs programs in nearly thirty languages. With thriving harbors opening onto the world's greatest ocean at the dawn of the Pacific Age, such diversity is likely to increase until that extraordinary hybrid glimpsed in the nineteenth century shall be realized in the twenty-first.

OVERLEAF:
THE SKY TRAIN IS VANCOUVER'S SLEEK ANSWER TO THE RAPID-TRANSIT NEEDS OF THE CITY'S GROWING POPULATION. THOUGH IT TRAVELS UNDERGROUND THROUGH THE CIVIC CORE, MOST OF ITS 16-MILE (25-KILOMETER) ROUTE FROM DOWNTOWN SOUTHEAST TO NEW WESTMINSTER IS ON ELEVATED TRACKS, PROVIDING SOME EXCELLENT METROPOLITAN VIEWS. HERE IT IS PASSING METROTOWN IN THE CITY OF BURNABY, BRITISH COLUMBIA.

PAGES 64–65:
SEATTLE'S SKYLINE AS SEEN FROM QUEEN ANNE HILL, WITH 14,410-FOOT MOUNT RAINIER OFF TO THE EAST.

THE EVOLUTION
OF VANCOUVER'S
ELEVATION IS
DRAMATIZED BY THE
JUXTAPOSITION OF
SEVERAL BUILDINGS
DOWNTOWN: SINCLAIR
CENTRE (FOREGROUND,
CONSTRUCTED AROUND
A 1910 POST OFFICE)
IS OVERSHADOWED
BY THE CITY'S FIRST
SKYSCRAPER, THE
ROYAL BANK TOWER
(1929), AND FINALLY
TOPPED BY THE
FUTURISTIC VANCOUVER
HARBOUR CENTRE
(COMPLETED IN 1977).

OPPOSITE:
BUILT ORIGINALLY
FOR SEATTLE'S 1962
CENTURY 21
EXPOSITION, THE SPACE
NEEDLE WAS MEANT TO
SYMBOLIZE THE CITY'S
POST—WORLD WAR II
SUCCESS. IT HAS SINCE
BECOME THE SKYLINE'S
MOST-RECOGNIZED
FEATURE, OFFERING
SPECTACULAR
PANORAMAS OF THE
CITY'S DOWNTOWN.
HERE, A WORKER
CHANGES LIGHTS ON
THE NEEDLE'S FLYING
SAUCER—LIKE TOP.

URBAN REFLECTIONS AT
THE INTERSECTION OF
ROBSON AND BURRARD
STREETS IN DOWNTOWN
VANCOUVER.

OPPOSITE:
ON THE NORTH SIDE OF
ROBSON SQUARE IN
VANCOUVER IS THE
PROVINCIAL LAW
COURTS BUILDING,
DESIGNED BY LOCAL
ARCHITECT ARTHUR
ERICKSON AND
COMPLETED IN 1979,
WITH A BLOCK-LONG
GLASS CANOPY THAT
LETS IN LOTS OF
SUMMER LIGHT BUT
PREVENTS CASCADIAN
RAINS FROM WETTING
ITS INHABITANTS'
LEGAL BRIEFS.
A STATUE OF
BLINDFOLDED LADY
JUSTICE PRESIDES
BENEATH THE
SKYLIGHT.

ABOVE:
LOOKING SOUTH FROM
THE WATERFALL AT
ROBSON SQUARE,
MODERN SKYSCRAPERS
RISE ABOVE SOME OF
THE CITY'S MOST
RECOGNIZABLE OLD
ARCHITECTURE. THE
PILLARED NEOCLASSICAL
STRUCTURE AT LEFT IS
THE 1912 VANCOUVER
ART GALLERY, ONCE THE
CITY'S COURTHOUSE.
IMMEDIATELY TO THE
LEFT OF THE GALLERY
RISES THE THIRD AND
MOST RECENT VERSION
OF THE GRAND HOTEL
VANCOUVER, OPENED
IN 1939.

BELOW:
THE ALWEG MONORAIL,
CARRYING PASSENGERS
DOWN FIFTH AVENUE
FROM SEATTLE CENTER
TO THE DOWNTOWN
SHIPPING HIVE OF
WESTLAKE CENTER,
WAS BUILT FOR THE
1962 WORLD'S FAIR.
SOME SEATTLEITES
HAVE SUGGESTED THAT
THE LINE BE EXTENDED,
WHILE OTHERS HAVE
ENCOURAGED THE
MONORAIL'S REMOVAL.
MEANWHILE, THIS
ONCE-FUTURISTIC
MASS-TRANSIT SYSTEM
REMAINS MUCH AS
PRESIDENT JOHN
KENNEDY SAW IT
DECADES AGO, A
CURIOSITY USED
MOSTLY BY TOURISTS.

OPPOSITE:
REPLETE WITH
HISTORICAL
ARCHITECTURAL
REFERENCES (FROM ITS
CRUCIFORM FLOOR
PLAN TO ITS STEPPED-
BACK PROFILE), THE
WASHINGTON MUTUAL
TOWER IS AN ELEGANT
DEPARTURE FROM A
GENERATION OF GLASS
BOXES RAISED IN
DOWNTOWN SEATTLE.

CASCADIA IS A REGION
OF BRIDGES:

ABOVE:
A STEEL ARCH BRIDGE
SPANS DECEPTION
PASS, BETWEEN
WHIDBEY AND FIDALGO
ISLANDS, NORTH
OF SEATTLE.
BELOW:
THE MERCER ISLAND
FLOATING BRIDGE,
GENERALLY CROWDED
WITH IMPATIENT
COMMUTERS ON
WEEKDAYS, CONNECTS
SEATTLE WITH ITS
RAPIDLY GROWING
SUBURBS ON THE
EAST SIDE OF LAKE
WASHINGTON.

ABOVE:
THE EVER-POPULAR CAPILANO SUSPENSION BRIDGE, LOCATED IN NORTH VANCOUVER'S CAPILANO RIVER REGIONAL PARK, IS THE MODERN VERSION OF A CEDAR-PLANK SPAN THAT WAS BUILT IN THE 1880S BY GEORGE GRANT MACKAY AND LOCAL NATIVE AMERICANS. WITH ITS VIEWS OF THE CANYON FROM 230 FEET (70 METERS) UP, IT IS DEFINITELY NOT FOR ACROPHOBES.

BELOW:
SEATTLEITES ARE ENTHUSIASTIC SUMMER BOATERS. IF THEY'RE NOT RUNNING THEIR CRAFT ON PUGET SOUND OR LAKE WASHINGTON, THEY MIGHT BE GLIMPSED BY DRIVERS OVER MOUNTLAKE BRIDGE AS THEY TRAVEL THROUGH THE EIGHT-MILE SHIP CANAL THAT HAS CONNECTED THOSE TWO BODIES OF WATER SINCE WORLD WAR I.

THE VICTORIAN
HERITAGE OF
TINY LaCONNER,
WASHINGTON, A
FORMER CANNING
VILLAGE NOW FAMOUS
FOR ITS ACCESS TO
POPULAR NEARBY
TULIP FIELDS, IS STILL
EVIDENT IN ITS
RESIDENTIAL
ARCHITECTURE.

OPPOSITE:
THE SLICK CITIES OF
SOUTHWESTERN
BRITISH COLUMBIA
STAND IN SHARP
CONTRAST TO
WILDERNESS OUTPOSTS
LIKE SULLIVAN BAY, A
FLOATING COMMUNITY
LOCATED UP THE COAST,
WHERE SEAPLANES AND
NEIGHBORING NATIVE
AMERICANS DROP
IN FOR FUEL AND
OTHER SUPPLIES.

ABOVE:
CASCADIA'S AFFECTION FOR ITS PLENTIFUL WATERS IS OBVIOUS IN THE MANY FLOATING-HOME COMMUNITIES IT HOSTS, SUCH AS THIS ONE ON FALSE CREEK, IN VANCOUVER.

BELOW:
SEATTLE'S FLOATING HOMES, LIKE THESE ON LAKE UNION, NEAR MOUNTLAKE BRIDGE, WERE ONCE ENDANGERED. NOW THEY'RE MUCH SOUGHT AFTER.

OPPOSITE:
AS PEACEFUL AS IT CAN BE TO LIVE IN A HOUSEBOAT IN SEATTLE OR VANCOUVER, IT'S NOTHING LIKE RESIDING IN THE FLOATING VILLAGE AT SULLIVAN BAY, BRITISH COLUMBIA.

ABOVE:

PIKE PLACE MARKET, SEATTLE'S FOREMOST AND QUIRKIEST PUBLIC SHOPPING COMPLEX, HAS BEEN AROUND SINCE 1907. BUT ITS SIGNATURE NEON CLOCK, UNDER WHICH REVELERS GATHER AT MIDNIGHT ON NEW YEAR'S EVE, DATES BACK ONLY TO THE 1920S OR 1930S.

BELOW:

EVER SEEN A FLOUNDER FLY? IT'S COMMON AT PIKE PLACE MARKET, WHERE SEAFOOD SALESPEOPLE SHOUT OUT NEW ORDERS, THEN FLING THE SELECTED FISH AT THE COUNTER TO BE WRAPPED AND RUNG UP.

THE MARKET IS A RIOT
OF COLOR, WHETHER
YOU'RE BUYING
WEDDING FLOWERS OR
SHOPPING THE STALLS
FOR FRUITS AND
VEGETABLES.

ONCE HOME TO
SMOKING, NOISY
INDUSTRIAL
OPERATIONS,
VANCOUVER'S
GRANVILLE ISLAND
(REALLY A NARROW-
NECKED PENINSULA)
LAY DERELICT
FOR YEARS BEFORE
THE CANADIAN
GOVERNMENT DECIDED
IN THE 1970S TO TURN
IT INTO A BOISTEROUS,
POLYCHROMATIC
SHOPPING AREA.
TODAY, IT IS ONE OF
THE CITY'S MOST
ATTRACTIVE VISITOR
DESTINATIONS.

ABOVE:
THE HEART OF THE
ISLAND IS THE PUBLIC
MARKET, WHERE YOU
CAN FIND EVERYTHING
FROM FARM-FRESH
PRODUCE TO HOT,
FRESH-BAKED COOKIES
AND FLAVORFUL SUSHI.

ABOVE:
A SIGN TUCKED
BENEATH THE
GRANVILLE STREET
BRIDGE HELPS DIRECT
SHOPPERS TO THE
EMPORIA, GALLERIES,
BREWERY, AND OTHER
BUSINESSES THAT KEEP
THE ISLAND HUSTLING.
BELOW AND
OPPOSITE BELOW:
YOUNGER BUYERS WHO
HEAD TO THE ISLAND'S
KIDS ONLY MARKET,
A TWO-STORY
DEPARTMENT STORE,
WILL FIND OFFERINGS
TO MARVEL AT SUCH AS
THOSE AVAILABLE IN
THE KITE STORE.

ABOVE:
STREETS THAT PASS
OVER SEATTLE'S MANY
HILLS, LIKE MAGNOLIA
BOULEVARD, OFFER
SOME STUNNING VIEWS
OF THE DOWNTOWN
SKYLINE.

BELOW:
BUILT IMMEDIATELY
AFTER SEATTLE'S
GREAT FIRE OF 1889,
ARCHITECT ELMER H.
FISHER'S PIONEER
BUILDING IS AN
EXCELLENT EXAMPLE
OF THE VICTORIAN
ROMANESQUE REVIVAL
ARCHITECTURE THAT
STILL DISTINGUISHES
THE PIONEER SQUARE
HISTORIC DISTRICT.
IN 1892, THE
AMERICAN INSTITUTE
OF ARCHITECTS
PROCLAIMED THIS
STRUCTURE "THE
FINEST BUILDING WEST
OF CHICAGO."

ABOVE:
"THE GATE TO THE NORTHWEST PASSAGE" IN VANCOUVER'S VANIER PARK, SOUTHWEST OF DOWNTOWN.

BELOW:
THOUGH ITS CANADIAN-ISRAELI ARCHITECT MOSHE SAFDIE DENIES THAT HIS INSPIRATION WAS THE ROMAN COLISEUM, HIS NEW VANCOUVER PUBLIC LIBRARY DEFINITELY EXUDES THE AUTHORITY AND GRANDEUR OF THAT ANCIENT STRUCTURE.

OPPOSITE:
KILLER WHALES, OR ORCAS, ARE OFTEN SEEN PLYING THE CASCADIAN WATERS. THEY'RE ALSO A HIT AT THE AQUARIUM IN VANCOUVER'S STANLEY PARK, LEAPING THROUGH THE AIR OR JUST WAVING THEIR TAILS AT PASSERSBY.
ABOVE:
AFTER BABY "QILA" WAS BORN TO ITS NINE-YEAR-OLD BELUGA WHALE MOTHER, "AURORA"—A RARE EVENT IN CAPTIVITY FOR THESE WHALES— VANCOUVER CHILDREN WERE IMMEDIATELY DRAWN TO THE SIGHT OF PARENT AND BABY EXPLORING THE DEPTHS OF THEIR TANK.

ONCE THE ESTATE OF GUY PHINNEY, A FLAMBOYANT ENGLISHMAN WHO MADE HIS FORTUNE IN CANADIAN REAL ESTATE, SEATTLE'S WOODLAND PARK ZOO HAS EVOLVED FROM A TYPICAL COMPOUND OF IRON BARS AND CONCRETE CAGES INTO A SPRAWLING COLLECTION OF EXCITING AND INNOVATIVE EXHIBITS.
CENTER:
ADDED DURING A MUTIMILLION-DOLLAR RENOVATION WAS AN ASIAN ELEPHANT FOREST, INCLUDING A REPLICA OF A THAI LOGGING CAMP, AND A SPACIOUS INDOOR VIEWING AREA WHERE THE ELEPHANTS WATCH FOR ADULTS AND CHILDREN BEARING SPECIAL FOOD SOLD ON THE ZOO GROUNDS.
BELOW:
A HIPPOPOTAMUS LOOKS BORED WITH THE SELECTION OF HUMANS FILING BACK AND FORTH NEAR ITS POND.

FISH AND FISHING ARE UBIQUITOUS SYMBOLS AT PUBLIC BUSINESSES AND INSTITUTIONS ACROSS CASCADIA.
ABOVE: THE AFISHIONADO GALLERY, AN ART GALLERY ON THE SEATTLE WATERFRONT, WHERE SEAFOOD ODORS CAN BE PUNGENT, DECLARES ITS DEVOTION TO THE DENIZENS OF THE DEEP.
CENTER: CHINOOK'S, A RESTAURANT AT FISHERMEN'S TERMINAL, BOASTS A MAJOR CATCH OF SEAFOOD ON ITS SIGNAGE.
BELOW: PERCHED ATOP AN EATERY ON THE SEATTLE WATERFRONT, THESE FISHERMEN ARE FROZEN IN A TABLEAU OF THEIR DAILY LABORS, DOOMED FOREVER TO BE AT SEA.

A COFFEE CUP IN THE HAND IS A CASCADIAN'S MODERN TALISMAN. ALMOST ANYWHERE YOU TRAVEL IN THE REGION, YOU'RE NEVER FAR FROM A CAFÉ OR A CONVENIENT "DRIVE-THRU" ESPRESSO STAND, LIKE THIS ONE IN SEATTLE.

BRITISH COLUMBIA'S ISLAND CAPITAL, VICTORIA, MAINTAINS ITS HISTORIC (AND MUCH-LOVED) BRITISHNESS WITH SUCH EVENTS AS AFTERNOON TEA AT THE ELEGANT EMPRESS HOTEL, WHICH OPENED IN 1908.

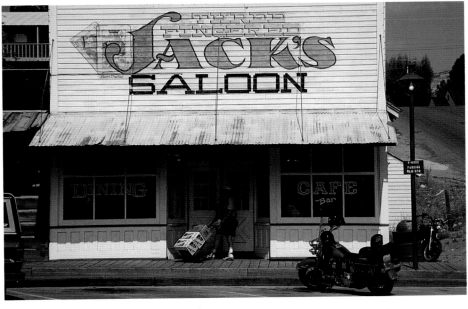

IN ORDER TO DRAW TRAVELERS, SMALL TOWNS ACROSS CASCADIA HAVE DEVELOPED CIVIC "THEMES." WINTHROP, IN CENTRAL WASHINGTON, FOR INSTANCE, USES PLACES LIKE THREE FINGERED JACK'S SALOON TO REINFORCE ITS WILD WEST IMAGE.

"CYBER-SIPPING" AT A COMPUTER CAFÉ IN VANCOUVER'S YALETOWN DISTRICT.

To experience a Bavarian village, one need only go as far as Leavenworth, in central Washington. A former sawmill town, Leavenworth long ago decided that it could capture plentiful tourist dollars by taking on a German alpine look. Now you can buy everything there from strudel to wool stocking caps.

ABOVE:
LaConner, Washington, makes the most of its association with tulip- and daffodil-growing by inviting visitors to take home some bulbs or seeds of their own. The Tillinghast Seed Company, at the entrance to town, is Cascadia's oldest mail-order seed store, dating back to 1885. Owner Alberta Lammers stands ready to take your order.

BELOW:
Cheerful daffodils and tulips at the Skagit Valley Bulb Farm, Washington.

OVERLEAF:
Washington's Skagit Valley (shown with snowcapped Mount Baker to the north) grows 75 percent of the state's commercial bulbs and exports tulips even to tulip-rich the Netherlands. The county's bulb industry now generates an astounding $12 million a year, and its annual Tulip Festival draws hundreds of thousands of people each April.

School of the Streets

Rick Anderson

Downtown Tommy shuffled along, feeling the hard pain of last night's bourbon. It stabbed his eyes with white needles and made tiny earthquakes in his chest. At 6 A.M., in a baseball cap and Hawaiian shirt, Tommy moved through Seattle to the door of the Rickshaw Restaurant off Pine Street. He flipped open the lock, dragged himself behind the bar, and poured a remedy of Jack Daniel's and soda. Balding, spare, a mild-mannered former television repairman who readily settled bar fights by snapping off the house lights and ducking, Tommy was in mid-swallow of his hangover relief when the naked man walked in.

Crapola, Tommy thought, it's one of those days.

"How do you do, sir," said the man, a mound of bare ivory, hatless and shoeless as well. He took the stool directly in front of Tommy.

"I can't serve you," Tommy said evenly, hands on the counter.

"Only want a beer."

"Can't do it."

The man sniffed. He raised his nose, indignant.

"Why not?" he said. *"Is it just because I'm naked?"*

"That's not it," Tommy sighed.

"Why then?"

"Because," said Tommy, "I know you don't got no money on you." The man blinked.

"And if you do," Tommy added, "I sure don't wanna touch it."

Mr. Naked departed into the beautiful sunrise. No fight, no cops, no damage. Tommy could have his headache in peace.

Such marvelous little stories once passed for commonplace on Seattle streets. But that, of course, was before the 1980s, when the whole town suddenly got the religion of tourism. It was before residents started to sanitize downtown, to elbow out the bars and flophouses and brothels that had made a drinking-man's-land out of Pioneer Square, Pike Place Market, Belltown, and the ribbon of concrete connecting them all, First Avenue. As the dives fronting the nation's original Skid Road (not Row) gave way to boutiques and hair salons and bright eateries, the inner city gained luster but lost some of its color.

Too many people today think of Seattle history as an old *caffè latte* stand. They forget that the city had remarkable character—and characters—long before it was "discovered" by the travel magazines.

Roll the Old Seattle footage...

At First and Pike, two drunk and angry woodsmen once dueled with chain saws on the street corner, fortunately running out of both alcohol and gasoline at the same time. In Pioneer Square, an Indian lassoed a passing Far West cab while shouting out impossible things about John Wayne's sex life.

A short, unwashed fellow named Backwards Louie left his mark on the city by walking local pavements not only drunk but always facing in the wrong direction. A well-known panhandler whom most folks went out of their way to avoid, Louie walked backward to give the impression that he was actually headed the other way. When an unsuspecting victim got close enough, Louie would wheel around and exclaim, "What a nice surprise! Got a quarter?"

Meanwhile, Sideways Dave trod Seattle streets sideways, never bothering to tell anyone why exactly, although everyone suspected he was just trying to avoid Backwards Louie.

Then there was Champion Olaf. A heavy-legged, bloodshot Norwegian who gave his heritage as "Scotch and soda," Olaf once ruled the bar stools downtown. Thanks to his fondness for the bottle, he was arrested 401 times in 25 years and collectively sentenced to 10,680 days for public drunkenness (though he actually served only 7,711 days in jail, or more than 20 years). "I saw it as always having a place to stay," Olaf explained.

And let's not forget Julius Meyers, who for years was considered the mayor of First Avenue, largely because he ran a famous store there, Meyers Music, where musician Quincy Jones's dad bought his son's first trumpet and Jimi Hendrix's dad bought his son's first guitar. Julius also earned his title because he stood out in dazzling contrast to his staggering constituency, an impeccably dressed gentleman among a merry band of pratfallers. He handled the street's public relations while the Downtown Tommys and a line of legendary Jim Beam Hall of Famers spilled cheap booze from one end of First to the other.

Together, these people and many others paraded out of the 1960s into the 1980s, leaving behind a cirrhotic trail of lounge history and wine stains.

But suddenly the Bowery faded. Then it was overthrown completely by gentrifiers, who turned classic buildings that nobody had wanted for decades into offices and apartments that locals ached to inhabit. In the transition, the old crowd was moved out. Frank the Box Man, who had lived in a packing crate on Fairview Avenue and each day donned two suits with three overcoats, appears to have escaped Earth's gravity. So has dapper Jack Theilman, who dwelt on Pike Street in an otherwise abandoned hundred-room hotel with his two roommates, a basketball-playing dog named Blackie and a walking catfish called Oscar. Also missing in action are George and Pansy Kotolaris, Seattle's only mother-son funeral-attending team. The squat, rosy-cheeked pair—Pansy dressed in flowered bonnets and George in second-hand suits—also attended weddings, baby christenings, and lavish parties to which they were not invited. They always brought a camera to take pictures of each other with the swells, smiling and snapping away long after they ran out of film. Pansy died a few years back. George went more recently, leaving no one behind to sit atop Pansy's grave, as he had done on her birthdays, keeping her spirit company as he watched baseball on a portable television set.

Even Downtown Tommy is holed up in a nursing home atop First Hill, wheelchair-bound from a stroke that also left him speechless. In an indignity that Tommy knows nothing about, his theater of the absurd, the Rickshaw, has been transformed into a tourist gift store specializing in trendy Doc Martens footwear.

Seattle is now a city aswagger, full of itself, no longer interested in people like Tommy. Although it has finally stopped wanting to be San Francisco, it now yearns instead to adopt the multiple virtues of Vancouver, which itself wants to be Hong Kong. Seattle isn't so much conscious of this desire as it is resigned to it, anticipating what seems to be the inevitable day when the Seattle and Vancouver city limits will meet.

The two towns have already been fused by history and environment. They each owe much to the timber and fishing industries, as well as to a couple of drunken founders: David ("Doc") Maynard in Seattle and John ("Gassy Jack") Deighton in Vancouver. (Say what you will, these are cities that respect liver disease.) Both have rocketing central towers, matchless harbors, silvery Northwest light, and that interchangeable Scandinavian/Canadian demeanor: insufferable niceness.

Seattle can't lay claim anymore, though, to a thoroughfare, like Vancouver's Davie Street, that is dominated by prostitutes, and progress has affected the street people on Elliott Bay to a much greater degree than it has changed the dissolute life on Vancouver's East Hastings Street. Yet for all the tax-sponsored cleanup, law-abiding Seattleites still don't feel safe on their downtown boulevards once the sun falls behind the Olympic Mountains. And the longer they stay away, the worse those streets become, left to the control of abusers. It's a vicious cycle, especially sad because nighttime is when the city's sidewalks can be most interesting, with revelers jamming the Belltown rock clubs, blues lovers on Ballard Avenue, the nose-ringed crowd swarming up Broadway, and college coeds mixing with junior-high dropouts along University Avenue.

Traveling on First Avenue, you find music and comedy clubs in Pioneer Square at the south and Belltown to the north. In between, at the crossroads of what might arguably be called the New Skid Road—a two-block radius of socially quarantined nightspots surrounding First and Pike Street, at the very doorstep of popular Pike Place Market—tourists and regulars mingle in such profusion that bewildered thieves wind up stealing from each other. This is downtown's current epicenter of weirdness. If you doubt that, you've not heard a wild, pint-size Scotsman named Andy Brodie tell about the day, a few years back, when a man called to his buddy crossing that intersection. "He yelled 'Hey, asshole!'" Brodie recalled, "and *everybody* in the street turned around."

The fun begins on Pike, in such places as the Turf Bar and its neighbor, the Mirror Tavern, hangers-on from the days when, if you wanted a new television set or a diamond ring, you bought it in the men's room. Among the latter-day purists of such traditions is Jack Coupon, a shadowy sort who buys up food stamps at half price from people who want the cash for drugs or drink. In one good stretch, he pocketed five hundred dollars worth of stamps for two hundred, then stocked up at the supermarket and went cruising on his girlfriend's yacht.

The most visible remnant of Seattle's bawdy past is just down the block, on First: the Lusty Lady, a dark, carpeted nudie joint boasting eleven live dance booths, twenty-one others with video monitors, and three 16-mm booths that still show the old

ARTIST RICHARD BEYER'S *PEOPLE WAITING FOR THE INTERURBAN*, LOCATED IN THE FREMONT NEIGHBORHOOD, IS ONE OF THE MOST-LOVED WORKS IN SEATTLE. THROUGHOUT THE SEASONS, LOCALS OUTFIT THIS MOTLEY CREW OF CAST-ALUMINUM FOLKS ANTICIPATING THE APPROACH OF PUBLIC TRANSPORT; YOU NEVER KNOW WHETHER THEY'LL BE DECKED OUT WITH WINTER CAPS, HALLOWEEN COSTUMES, OR EVEN NEW YEAR'S DIAPERS.

OVERLEAF:
VANCOUVER BOASTS THE SECOND-LARGEST (AFTER SAN FRANCISCO) CHINESE COMMUNITY IN NORTH AMERICA. ALTHOUGH ITS INFLUENCE EXTENDS TO ALL QUARTERS OF THE CITY, IT IS MOST CONCENTRATED IN CHINATOWN, WHERE CAN BE FOUND THE CHINESE CULTURAL CENTRE AND THE SMALL DR. SUN YAT-SEN CLASSICAL CHINESE GARDEN (MODELED AFTER A MING DYNASTY GARDEN IN SU-CHOU, KIANGSU PROVINCE).

X-rated loops. Any claim that Washington's largest city makes of thoroughgoing wholesomeness is belied by the Lady's annual take—about $2 million. How has this joint survived while most of its competitors folded up their tents a long time ago? Operator Jude Cade, a willowy, bespectacled fifty-something feminist who once worked as the executive secretary at an oil company, has discovered that nudity, money, and respect are not mutually exclusive. Dressed in a smart, ankle-length executive suit, she explained this while sitting in her office, filled with computers and fax machines, just a few steps away from the writhing naked dancers.

Its location directly across the street from the grand Seattle Art Museum may also help Cade's business. Her dance parlor enjoys some modest propriety in the museum's shadow, and the Lady's naughty-but-nice marquee makes SAM seem a tad less stuffy. Every day, Cade and her crew demonstrate their sense of humor on that hot-pink message board. Cade even holds contests for the best innuendo-filled marquee sayings, attracting entries from nearby office workers, including female employees of Nordstrom. Unfortunately, she has had to throw out some of the Nordstrom suggestions. "I liked them," she said, "but some weren't politically correct. I mean, every business has its standards."

It's a funny notion, being politically correct on Skid Road. But times change— though if today you stood at First and Pike and shouted "Hey, asshole!" you might be surprised to discover they haven't changed all that much.

THE INTERNATIONAL FLAVORS OF GREATER VANCOUVER ARE BOTH RICH AND DIVERSE. JUST SOUTH OF THE CITY, IN THE COMMUNITY OF RICHMOND, BUDDHISTS GATHER TO SHARE SPIRITUAL WISDOM AND PRAY AT A HIGHLY DECORATED TEMPLE.

COLORFUL BANNERS
AND STREETLIGHTS
DECORATE
VANCOUVER'S
CHINATOWN, ONE OF
THE LARGEST
NEIGHBORHOODS OF
ITS KIND IN
NORTH AMERICA.

THE EXCEPTIONAL
FILIPINO DANCE
COMPANY CELEBRATES
SEATTLE'S LONG
ASIAN TIES AT THE
CHINATOWN FESTIVAL.

ABOVE:
EASTER SERVICES ARE
A GRAND AFFAIR AT
SEATTLE'S ST. JAMES
CATHEDRAL, AN
ASTONISHING NEO-
BAROQUE STRUCTURE
MOST RECOGNIZABLE
FOR ITS TWIN 175-FOOT
TOWERS.

BELOW:
CASCADIA IS SUCH A
YOUNG PLACE
HISTORICALLY THAT ITS
FOREIGN ROOTS STILL
LIE NEAR ITS SURFACE.
IN VICTORIA, STREET
HAWKERS (THIS ONE
PROMOTING A POPULAR
LOCAL CHOCOLATIER)
MAY DRESS AS ENGLISH
BEEFEATERS.

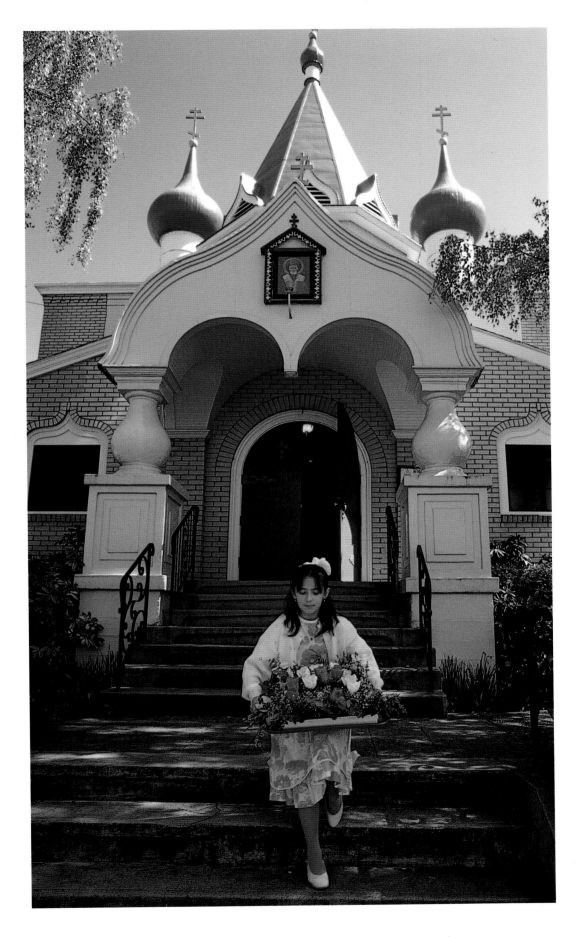

THE MINISTER'S
DAUGHTER HELPS OUT
AT ST. SPIRIDON
ORTHODOX CHURCH,
WHICH CARRIES ON A
TRADITION OF RUSSIAN
ORTHODOX WORSHIP IN
SEATTLE THAT DATES
BACK AS FAR AS 1898.

PIKE PLACE MARKET
HELPS FILL NOT
ONLY SEATTLE'S
REFRIGERATORS BUT
ITS ENTERTAINMENT
NEEDS AS WELL. ON
SUNNY DAYS, VISITORS
MIGHT FIND SQUARE
DANCERS HOLDING
FORTH IN THE STREET
(ABOVE) OR MUSICIANS
PLAYING FOR THEIR
SUPPER ON THE
SIDEWALK (BELOW).

IN CASCADIA, THE NATIVE AMERICAN PRESENCE IS STILL KEENLY FELT, PARTICULARLY IN BRITISH COLUMBIA.
ABOVE: SOMETIMES THIS PRESENCE IS QUIETLY EXERTED, AS IN THIS BURIAL GROUND ON ECHO BAY.
BELOW: BUT FIRST NATIONS PEOPLE—AS MEMBERS OF THE MUSQUEAM, SQUAMISH, AND OTHER TRIBES ARE KNOWN TODAY—ALSO KEEP THEIR TRADITIONS VITAL WITH LIVELY FESTIVALS. AT THIS FIRST NATIONS EVENT IN VICTORIA, DRUMMERS FILL THE BRIGHT DAY WITH CHEERFUL RHYTHMS.

CASCADIA HAS ALWAYS PLAYED A KEY ROLE IN INTERNATIONAL AFFAIRS.
ABOVE: COSTUMED COMBATANTS RECALL THE FAMOUS PIG WAR OF 1859, WHEN BRITISH AND U.S. TROOPS ALMOST CAME TO BLOWS ON WASHINGTON'S SAN JUAN ISLAND AFTER AN ENGLISH HOG WANDERED ONTO AN AMERICAN FARMER'S PROPERTY.
BELOW: TODAY, THE REGION IS INTEGRAL TO MAINTAINING PEACE ALL OVER THE PACIFIC RIM, SERVING AS A BASE FOR MILITARY PERSONNEL, SUCH AS THESE CANADIAN STEALTH FIGHTER PILOTS MUGGING FOR THE CAMERA AT THE ABBOTSFORD INTERNATIONAL AIR SHOW IN BRITISH COLUMBIA.

SOME PEOPLE WEAR
THEIR NATIONAL PRIDE
ON THEIR SLEEVES.
OTHERS, LIKE THIS
MOTHER AND DAUGHTER
WHO ARE CELEBRATING
THE FOURTH OF JULY AT
ROCHE HARBOR, ON
WASHINGTON'S SAN
JUAN ISLAND, PREFER
TO MAKE A SOMEWHAT
BROADER STATEMENT.

ABOVE:
RUNNERS, ROLLERBLADERS, AND LOVERS ARE THE MOST COMMON USERS OF THE MAIN PATH THAT SURROUNDS SEATTLE'S GREEN LAKE. ACTING ON THE ADVICE OF THE RENOWNED OLMSTED BROTHERS LANDSCAPING FIRM OF MASSACHUSSETTS, IN 1911 THE CITY LOWERED THE WATER LEVEL, EXPOSING NEW LAND ON WHICH A LAKEFRONT PARK COULD BE BUILT. THOUSANDS OF PEOPLE NOW USE THE PATHS, TENNIS COURTS, AND BASKETBALL COURTS AROUND THE WATER. UNFORTUNATELY, FEW PEOPLE SWIM THERE, SINCE BY LOWERING THE LAKE LEVEL, PLANNERS ALSO ELIMINATED THE NATURAL SPRINGS AND CREEKS THAT ONCE KEPT IT FRESH AND FREE OF ITCH-PROVOKING ALGAE. BALD EAGLES SOMETIMES COME TO REST AT THE LAKE'S NORTH END.

BELOW:
IT DOESN'T TAKE MUCH TO GET AWAY FROM IT ALL IN CASCADIA. HERE, A MAN PUTS IN SOME HAMMOCK REST OFF HIS BOAT, WHICH IS DOCKED IN PRINCESS LOUISA INLET, IN MALASPINA STRAIT, OUTSIDE OF POWELL RIVER, BRITISH COLUMBIA.

CASCADIANS KNOW
NOTHING IF NOT HOW
TO RELAX.
ABOVE:
LADIES IN THEIR
SUMMER HATS CHAT
ALONG THE SHORES OF
ENGLISH BAY, SOUTH
OF DOWNTOWN
VANCOUVER.
BELOW:
A MORE URBAN
HANGOUT IS THE PLAZA
AT SEATTLE'S
WESTLAKE CENTER,
WHERE A CONVENIENT
SOURCE OF CAFFEINE
KEEPS PEOPLE FROM
FALLING ASLEEP IN THIS
TRANQUIL SETTING.

OVERLEAF:
VISITING CASCADIA IN
THE 1880S, BRITISH
AUTHOR RUDYARD
KIPLING REMARKED,
"SUCH A LAND IS GOOD
FOR AN ENERGETIC
MAN," BUT ADDED, "IT
IS ALSO NOT SO BAD
FOR THE LOAFER."
INDEED, THE
OPPORTUNITIES FOR
SOME QUALITY
DOWNTIME ABOUND IN
THESE PARTS,
INCLUDING TAKING A
SUNSET STROLL
BEFORE A BEACHFRONT
WILDERNESS CABIN
AT ECHO BAY,
BRITISH COLUMBIA.

Borderline Art

Roger Downey

Early last summer, a friend and I met on Seattle's Capitol Hill to catch a play—a multi-media, theater-of-testimony staging of a Euripides tragedy we'd heard good things about. We had arrived early, and the night was far too balmy to take our seats in an un-air-conditioned church hall any sooner than we had to, so we spent some time amid the continuous parade down Broadway Avenue, strolling with the grannies, grungers, street mohawks, hippies (as perfectly preserved as flies in amber), stray dogs, drag queens, and young people on skateboards.

We dropped in on an international newsstand for a while, stared through the windows of a gay-and-lesbian bookstore, thought about stopping at Starbucks for an iced latte but agreed we'd already had too much coffee, and ended up sitting behind the window of the Gravity Bar, sipping organic fruit-and-yogurt smoothies and contemplating the passing sidewalk show.

Beside us, two teenage girls were chatting, one looking as prim as a denizen of Miss Annie Wright's academy for young Seattle ladies, the other rainbow-haired and liberally pierced.

"I won't be able to come to the Dead concert," I overheard the prim one say, sounding desolate. "Next week we're going to Europe for two months."

"Oh, *no*, kiddie, what a *bummer*," her pierced friend commiserated. "What *for*?"

My first thought, of course, was: "These kids today!" But my second thought was, "Well, now, she's got a point." Growing up in Spokane, Washington, in the 1950s, I would have killed to be taken to Europe for two *weeks*, let alone two months. And Europe still has a lot going for it, as befits a place with a two-thousand-year head start in the culture department. But these days I spend time on both sides of the Atlantic, and it's been a long while since I felt, in returning to Seattle, that I was headed back to the boonies.

It was not always so. When I arrived at Seattle in 1964, this place looked pretty bush, even to a high-school graduate country boy back from two and a half years in Europe with the United States Army. The world's fair (the Elvis one) had concluded just a year or so earlier, and the city was still stunned by its success, but about the only new sign of sophistication I could see was the Space Needle, and both Stockholm and Frankfurt had taller revolving restaurants.

The Seattle Symphony Orchestra no longer played in a downtown movie theater; the fair had given birth to a fledgling opera company, and even a resident classic-theater company on the European model. However, there was no ballet company, few museums, above all no cultural *life*. Seattle had served most of its first fifty years as a place from which to ship logs out to boomtown San Francisco or as a staging ground for the Yukon and Alaska gold rushes. A lot of Seattleites made a lot of money in those days, yet unlike the proud money of New York, Philadelphia, or Pittsburgh, they didn't spend it on culture—at least not at home.

The Seattle culture scene was a little backward; it was left for enthusiasts and amateurs to dabble in. Wealthy geologist Dr. Richard Fuller all but single-handedly acquired a world-class collection of Oriental art, and then he was graciously allowed to present the city with a world-class building in which to house it (architect Carl Gould's old Seattle Art Museum [SAM]—now the Asian Art Museum—at Volunteer Park). Meanwhile, Miss Nellie Cornish kept the flame alive at her homemade arts conservatory up on Capitol Hill (today's Cornish Art Institute). The best people could only smile at art and artists they didn't yet understand. "My husband says our daughter can paint better than that Mark Tobey," one local matron might tell another at a cocktail party, "and I don't call what that Cunningham person does *dancing*, do you?"

This antiprovincial brand of provincialism survived well into the 1950s; in the world of the arts, Seattle was best known as a town many admired artists came *from*. After the 1962 world's fair, with John F. Kennedy in the White House and the arts in the air, those first self-conscious cultural plantings began to take root and spread. The Seattle Repertory Theater's focus on classics gave rise to an equally focused rival, A Contemporary Theater (ACT). Thanks to the Seattle Opera's need for a first-rate pit orchestra, there was finally enough work for classically trained musicians to make the Seattle Symphony a full-time ensemble; the Seattle Opera's need for dancers in time spawned the Pacific Northwest Ballet (PNB).

Twenty years after the fair, formerly arts-poor Seattle found itself one of the few cities in America with a full-time symphony, opera, and ballet, as well as half a dozen theaters.

By the end of the 1980s, the Seattle Symphony had toured Europe, Seattle Rep shows had ended up on Broadway, and PNB dancers had performed at the Kennedy Center in Washington, D.C. Seattle was beginning to take the arts for granted. And that, on the whole, boded well. In the same way that good wine, good coffee, and good bread had come to be taken for granted, art was no longer considered a luxury but a staple, a basic ingredient of civic life, and when buying staples, insisting on quality signals not snobbery but plain common sense.

The quality is there now. Children grow up on it: Every year a good ten thousand of them go with their parents to see Pacific Northwest Ballet's *Nutcracker*. Seattle Opera has mounted Richard Wagner's wonderful, absurd, over-the-top four-evening extravaganza, *The Ring of the Nibelung*, not once but *four* times over the last ten years, with more and more local people, young and old, in the audience with each outing. And maybe neither Wendy Wasserstein's *The Sisters Rosensweig* nor Neil Simon's *London Suite* can compare with *King Lear*, exactly, but how good it feels as a Seattleite, when some New Yorker is mouthing off about one of those plays, to be able to say, "Oh, yes, I saw the world premiere a few years ago back home."

Even those who never go near Seattle's palaces of high culture benefit from their flourishing existence. In no area is this truer than in theater. During the 1970s, a legend spread through the American theater community that Seattle was "a real theater town." By the end of the 1980s so many topflight artists had moved within easy access of Elliott Bay that the legend turned true. The established houses could not provide enough work to keep all the artists interested and busy, so they started putting on their own shows, in lofts, basements, and storefronts all over town.

Many of these "fringe" productions are just as marginal as the term implies; a surprising number prove as good as theater gets. Much of this "fringe" work, too, is "avant-garde," in the best and worst senses of that term; but an amazing number of these pieces, "avant-garde" or not, offer "theater for everybody," as rowdy and rousing and involving as that offered by the big houses, and then some.

Historically, Seattle has always been "a theater town." During the Klondike gold rush days, a dozen local repertory companies performed the kind of shows that appealed to a brawling, working-class, boomtown audience. It was such a perfect audience sample that two of the nation's top vaudeville circuits tried out their acts here. For some reason, that kind of "pop" edge hangs on in Seattle culture. The arts here don't have to be "fine" to be fine with us.

When it comes to the movies, that all-American pop entertainment, Seattleites have an appetite for film that's well out of proportion to their numbers. Most screenings at the annual Seattle International Film Festival fill to bursting (even for seven-hour Hungarian epics about pornography in 1960s Budapest), and distributors have long known that worthy but oddball films needing delicate handling are assured of getting a fair shake from Seattle audiences. There's a thriving independent-film and -video scene here, too, and Hollywood movie crews often clutter up the streets, though they're mostly just shooting exteriors and scenery for films to be made in the main elsewhere. Only recently has Seattle become serious about promoting itself as a good place to shoot entire films. That puts it far behind Vancouver, which has already established itself as a top production center for films and episodic television.

Vancouver is Seattle's great cultural rival in numerous ways, and until recently, the race between the towns was neck and neck, or perhaps tipped toward the city on Burrard Inlet. Arts groups in Vancouver enjoyed generous support from federal, provincial, and city authorities; big-time international tours—the Royal Ballet, Andrew Lloyd Webber's *The Phantom of the Opera*—played long runs in the city while stiffing Seattle entirely.

But the arts have flagged in Vancouver. Its opera, once a major contender, has slumped; its symphony has lost its luster; nonprofit theater, once thriving, is struggling to hang on in the city. You can still catch first-class touring events at the magnificent Queen Elizabeth Theatre downtown, and the doughty bunch that runs the Arts Club Theatre still cranks out production after production (though mostly of work—shades of Second City TV's *Great White North!*—almost comically high in "Canadian content").

For years, only the fabulous collection of Northwest Coast Indian art housed at the University of British Columbia could claim world-class status on the Vancouver cultural scene. That only changed in recent memory with the opening of the city's new Ford Theatre and its neighbor, the whimsically grandiose Central Library (both designed by Canadian-Israeli architect Moshe Safdie). They are a one-two cultural punch of which Vancouver can be justly proud.

The downtown Seattle Art Museum has a respectable collection of Coast Indian art, too, but it's not remotely in Vancouver's league. Neither is SAM focused on high-art holdings. The best collection in the Robert Venturi–designed building is an assembly of African masks, robes, and furnishings—stunning works, if not in the high-toned European artistic tradition.

No problem. Seattleites like their art robust, strong-flavored, unpretentious.

Consider "grunge" rock. It took the continent by surprise when it blew out of Seattle around 1990. Locals weren't surprised, though; they'd been familiar with grunge's raucous sound, aggressive stance, and distinctive thrift-shop couture for close to a decade.

The boundaries between high and pop culture are just as blurred elsewhere in the local arts scene. Musicians who flail away in Belltown clubs each weekend may turn up on off nights playing with the Young Composers Collective or doing backup for a Sam Shepard staging at New City Theater. Although Seattle has its share of "serious" visual artists and galleries, its most distinctive products are, on one side, the sumptuous, gloriously baroque glass sculptures created by Dale Chihuly and his many students and followers; and on the other side, wholly pop-culturish comic-strip art, from all-but-mainstream artists like Lynda ("Ernie Pook's Comeek") Barry and Gary ("The Far Side") Larson to the dozens of deliberately grungy, often scurrilous pensters of the Fantagraphics school.

"Public art" has been defined as "something expensive, ugly, and useless that you pay for whether you want to or not." Seattle has its share of that kind of public art, along with a few beloved masterworks, such as Henry Moore's giant-dinosaur-bone assemblage on a Fourth Avenue plaza downtown and Barnett Newman's soaring, tragic *Broken Obelisk* on the University of Washington campus. But the public reserves its deepest affection for funky local treasures like the collectively created *Fremont Troll* (under the north end of the Aurora Bridge); Rich Beyer's carved-concrete commuter still life *People Waiting for the Interurban*; and Jack Mackie's bronze-inset dance-step instructions in the sidewalks along Broadway.

Back in the early 1970s, some local arts boosters persuaded the city to sponsor a Labor Day weekend arts festival at Seattle Center. Within a year or two, the celebration had metamorphosed from a rather upscale operation into a three-day civic party, its all-inclusive nature indicated by the name that came to stick to it: Bumbershoot. Lovers of the more serious arts have always disapproved of this festival's emphasis on megapop and mass-market acts, but there's no question that Bumbershoot captures, for better or worse, Seattle's artistic soul. And when, in 1995, the headline event was a memorial concert for favorite musical son Jimi Hendrix, featuring some dozen rock greats who paid him tribute, the distinction between high and low culture was blown to hell—much to the delight of Seattleites. This was art in the service of life; no need to read the label.

OVERLEAF:
SEATTLE'S VOLUNTEER PARK CONSERVATORY ON CAPITOL HILL, CONSTRUCTED IN 1912, WAS BASED ON THE DESIGN OF LONDON'S 1851 CRYSTAL PALACE. TODAY, MORE THAN A QUARTER OF A MILLION VISITORS ANNUALLY STUDY THE GREENHOUSE'S ARRAY OF ORCHIDS, CACTI, AND TROPICAL SPECIES.

PAGES 118–19:
THE GREAT GALLERY AT SEATTLE'S MUSEUM OF FLIGHT IS FILLED WITH BIPLANES, MILITARY AIRCRAFT, AND EVEN A GIANT DC-13, ALL OF WHICH HELP ADULTS AND YOUNGSTERS TO LEARN MORE ABOUT HOW HUMANS TURNED THEIR DREAM OF FLYING INTO FACT. ALTHOUGH IT IS LOCATED AT BOEING FIELD, SOUTH OF DOWNTOWN, THE MUSEUM IS ACTUALLY AN INDEPENDENT OPERATION.

PREVIOUS PAGES: SCULPTOR JONATHAN BOROFSKY'S 48-FOOT KINETIC ARTWORK *HAMMERING MAN* GREETS VISITORS TO THE DOWNTOWN SEATTLE ART MUSEUM, A HIGHLY REGARDED BUILDING BY ARCHITECT ROBERT VENTURI.

LEFT: ONE OF THE FINEST SPACES IN THE SEATTLE ART MUSEUM IS THE GRAND STAIRCASE, LEADING FROM THE LOBBY TO THE SECOND-FLOOR GALLERIES AND PUNCTUATED BY SCULPTURES OF CHINESE MILITARY GUARDIANS, CAMELS, AND RAMS.

OPPOSITE: CREATED FOR SEATTLE'S 1962 WORLD'S FAIR BY LOCALLY BORN ARCHITECT MINORU YAMASAKI (WHO LATER DESIGNED THE TWIN TOWERS OF MANHATTAN'S WORLD TRADE CENTER), THE PACIFIC SCIENCE CENTER REMAINS A CENTERPIECE AT THE OLD FAIR SITE, SINCE RE-CREATED AS SEATTLE CENTER. THE STUNT BICYCLE IN THE MAIN COURTYARD IS PART OF A COLLECTION FROM THE CHILDREN'S DISCOVERY MUSEUM, HOUSED IN THE CENTER.

You won't find the almighty Oz, or Dorothy and Toto, too, but the Tin Man from *The Wizard of Oz* puts in a heartfelt appearance at Seattle's Children's Discovery Museum.

OPPOSITE:
An acrobatic bicycle sculpture left over from Vancouver's Expo '86.

DALE CHIHULY, HAILED AS THE FINEST GLASS SCULPTOR OF THE TWENTIETH CENTURY, STARTED OUT IN INTERIOR DESIGN. HE HAPPENED ON GLASSBLOWING BY ACCIDENT, WHILE PLAYING WITH SOME STAINED GLASS HE HAD MELTED IN A KILN ONE NIGHT. "I DIPPED A STEEL PIPE INTO IT, BLEW INTO THE PIPE, AND A BUBBLE OF GLASS APPEARED," HE ONCE TOLD *SEATTLE* MAGAZINE. "I'D NEVER SEEN GLASSBLOWING BEFORE." HE HAS SINCE HELPED DEVELOP THE PILCHUCK GLASS SCHOOL IN STANWOOD, WASHINGTON, AND MADE SEATTLE A CENTER OF GLASSBLOWING TO RIVAL VENICE. WORK HE HAS CREATED HIMSELF OR, MORE OFTEN THESE DAYS (OWING TO A 1976 CAR ACCIDENT THAT BLINDED HIM IN ONE EYE), WORK THAT HE HAS SUPERVISED APPEARS IN MANY MAJOR BUILDINGS AROUND CASCADIA.

PREVIOUS PAGES: CHIHULY GLASS SCULPTURES COMMAND ATTENTION AT A TACOMA ART MUSEUM EXHIBIT IN THAT CITY'S BEAUTIFULLY REFURBISHED 1911 UNION STATION.

LEFT: CHIHULY'S *MONARCH WINDOW* AT UNION STATION SHOWS THE GLASS FLOWERS THAT HAVE BECOME ONE OF HIS SIGNATURE ITEMS.

OPPOSITE: GLASSBLOWING AT THE PILCHUCK GLASS SCHOOL IS ALMOST A SACRED ENDEAVOR.

ABOVE:
RICHARD WAGNER'S HARD-TO-STAGE *THE RING OF THE NIBELUNG* HAS BEEN PRESENTED SO MANY TIMES OVER THE LAST DECADE BY THE SEATTLE OPERA THAT IT HAS FINALLY BECOME FAIR GAME FOR SPOOFING. HERE THE ACT THEATER COMPANY PRESENTS ITS OWN VERSION, TITLED *DAS BARBECUE*.

CENTER:
YOUNG PUPILS OF THE ACCLAIMED PACIFIC NORTHWEST BALLET SCHOOL PRACTICE THEIR STRETCHING AND BALANCING ON A WEEKEND MORNING AT SEATTLE CENTER.

BELOW:
AFTER YEARS OF LANGUISHING IN THE SHADOW OF SEATTLE, VANCOUVER IS REINVIGORATING ITS ARTS SCENE. INTEGRAL TO THAT ENDEAVOR HAS BEEN THE OPENING OF THE MOSHE SAFDIE—DESIGNED FORD CENTRE FOR THE PERFORMING ARTS; EVEN THE ROTUNDA OF ITS THEATER HAS A THEATRICAL DRAMA TO IT.

SEATTLE THEATER
KNOWS FEW BOUNDS.
A COMPANY CALLED
ON THE BOARDS
EMPLOYED A TRAPEZE
IN ITS PRODUCTION
OF *RAPTURE RUMI*,
CHOREOGRAPHED BY
ROBERT DAVIDSON.

It's sometimes necessary to look twice in Cascadia just to be sure that the people you see in your peregrinations are not really statuary.

ABOVE:
What appear to be a mother and child hanging out on a sunny day are actually wood sculptures decorating a floating home on Seattle's Lake Union.
BELOW:
Bronze children play leapfrog at Marina Park in Kirkland, an Eastside suburb.

A BOY AND HIS DOG, CREATED BY SCULPTOR GEORGIA GERBER, TAKE IN THE PEACEFUL ENVIRONS OF LANGLEY, A TOWN ON WASHINGTON'S WHIDBEY ISLAND.

OVERLEAF: LIKE SOME BROTHERS GRIMM LEGEND BROUGHT FORTH IN SCULPTURE, THE OMINOUS FREMONT TROLL HIDES BENEATH THE NORTH END OF THE GEORGE WASHINGTON MEMORIAL BRIDGE (BETTER KNOWN AS THE AURORA BRIDGE), NOT FAR NORTH OF DOWNTOWN SEATTLE. A COMMUNITY PROJECT FROM THE FREMONT ARTS COUNCIL, THE TROLL WAS CREATED IN 1990 FROM FERROCONCRETE, WITH A REAL VOLKSWAGEN BEETLE CLUTCHED IN ITS LEFT FIST. IT'S A POPULAR CLIMBING SPOT FOR YOUNGSTERS.

ABOVE LEFT:
THE BRITISH EMPIRE
MAY HAVE CRUMBLED,
BUT QUEEN VICTORIA
REMAINS UNFLUSTERED
IN FRONT OF THE NEO-
GOTHIC PARLIAMENT
BUILDING IN VICTORIA,
BRITISH COLUMBIA.

BELOW LEFT:
LADY JUSTICE
HOPES THAT HER
PRESENCE WILL KEEP
LAWYERS HONEST AT
VANCOUVER'S
PROVINCIAL LAW
COURTS BUILDING,
DESIGNED BY LOCAL
ARCHITECT ARTHUR
ERICKSON.

OPPOSITE ABOVE RIGHT: JAMES A. WEHN DESIGNED THE DRINKING FOUNTAIN AND BUST OF CHIEF SEALTH THAT NOW DRAW SO MUCH ATTENTION AT SEATTLE'S PIONEER PLACE PARK, RIGHT IN THE HEART OF PIONEER SQUARE (AT FIRST AVENUE AND YESLER WAY). THE PIECE WAS INSTALLED IN 1909. ANOTHER WEHN TRIBUTE TO THE CITY'S NAMESAKE, THIS ONE A FULL-BODY RENDITION, STANDS AT TILLIKUM PLACE, AT FIFTH AVENUE AND CEDAR STREET, ALSO IN SEATTLE.

OPPOSITE BELOW RIGHT: *SEATTLE FISHERMEN'S MEMORIAL* WAS CREATED BY RONALD W. PETTY TO HONOR THE HUNDREDS OF SEATTLE-AREA COMMERCIAL FISHERMEN WHO HAVE DIED OR BEEN LOST WHILE TRYING TO REAP CASCADIA'S SEAFOOD BOUNTY. THE STATUE STANDS ATOP A 30-FOOT COLUMN AT FISHERMEN'S TERMINAL, IN THE MAGNOLIA NEIGHBORHOOD. AT THE BASE OF THE COLUMN IS A VARIETY OF SEA CREATURES SANDBLASTED ONTO GLASS BRICK BY SEATTLE ARTIST PETER DAVID.

RELAXING AT VANCOUVER'S EXPO '86.

ABOVE:
THE TOWERS OF A ONCE-BELCHING GAS COMPANY PLANT HAVE BEEN TURNED INTO SURPRISINGLY PEACEFUL GAS WORKS PARK, AT THE NORTH END OF SEATTLE'S LAKE UNION. KITE ENTHUSIASTS AND PICNICKERS SHOW UP WHERE ONLY MEN IN HARD HATS ONCE TROD, AND GRAFFITI ARTISTS HAVE ADDED THEIR OWN CONTRIBUTIONS TO WHAT REMAINS OF THE INDUSTRIAL HULKS.

BELOW:
MODERN ART PUNCTUATES MANY OF THE GREENSWARDS AND SHORES OF VANCOUVER'S STANLEY PARK. THIS PIECE IS CALLED *SEARCH*.

OPPOSITE:
A SCULPTURE IN PIONEER SQUARE, SEATTLE.

OVERLEAF:
PRIMAVERA II BREAKS THE MONOTONY OF DRIVING OVER INTERSTATE 90. IT APPEARS ON AN OVERPASS ON MERCER ISLAND, EAST OF SEATTLE.

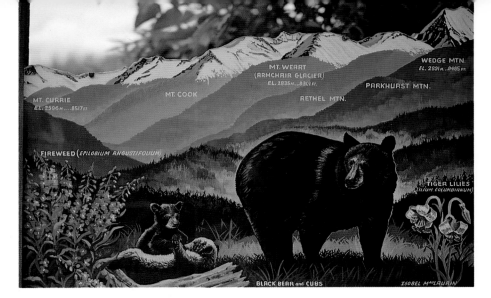

CASCADIANS ARE GREAT ONES FOR COVERING PUBLIC WALLS WITH ART.

AT ALTA LAKE, NEAR THE BRITISH COLUMBIA TOWN OF WHISTLER, A NATURAL-HISTORY MURAL DECORATES A WALL IN RAINBOW PARK.

A SEATTLE PLAYGROUND MURAL CELEBRATES THE CITY'S ASIAN HERITAGE.

THE SIGNAGE ON A MILK COMPANY IN SEATTLE MAKES UDDER FUN OF COMMERCE.

STUDENTS AT LORD TENNYSON PUBLIC SCHOOL ON VANCOUVER'S GRANVILLE ISLAND TOOK UP BRUSHES AND LEFT A PAINTED LEGACY CALLED *A CHILD'S VISION OF THE FUTURE.*

OPPOSITE: SEATTLE'S BUS COMPANY SPENT ABOUT $3 MILLION FOR ARTWORK TO ENLIVEN THE FIVE UNDERGROUND STOPS ALONG ITS DOWNTOWN BUS TUNNEL. THIS WALL OF DECORATIVE TILES, MADE BY FOURTH- AND FIFTH-GRADERS FROM THE BEACON HILL AND BAILEY GATZERT SCHOOLS, DECORATES THE INTERNATIONAL DISTRICT STOP.

No, they're not strings of Christmas lights. They're markers on nets that have been piled up at Fishermen's Terminal in Seattle.

OPPOSITE:
Seattle's variation on the sidewalk-decoration theme—unlike the star-studded but static Walk of Fame in Hollywood—can literally sweep you off your feet. These inlaid bronze steps by local artist Jack Mackie teach couples a variety of classic dances. They are found on Capitol Hill, lining both sides of Broadway between East Pine and East Roy streets. Mambo, anyone?

ABOVE:
BLAKE ISLAND, JUST WEST ACROSS PUGET SOUND FROM SEATTLE, IS A FAVORITE DESTINATION FOR OUT-OF-TOWNERS (PRESIDENT CLINTON EVEN LED A CONTINGENT OF PACIFIC RIM LEADERS THERE). THE BIRTHPLACE OF CHIEF SEALTH, IT REMAINS THE SITE OF NATIVE AMERICAN CEREMONIES. A SALMON FEAST, RE-CREATING SALMON BAKES AND POTLATCHES THAT DEFINED INDIAN CULTURE HERE FOR CENTURIES, DRAWS VISITORS WHO LISTEN TO MUSIC WHILE THEY WAIT MORE OR LESS PATIENTLY IN LINE FOR ENTRY INTO THE ISLAND'S EVENTS LODGE.

BELOW:
NATIVE AMERICAN IMAGERY SEEMS ALSO TO HAVE BEEN PICKED UP IN A MURAL SEEN MOSTLY BY SEATTLE'S LARGE HOMELESS POPULATION.

JAPANESE CHILDREN
TAKE IN THE SUNSHINE
BENEATH A DRAGON
MURAL IN SEATTLE'S
INTERNATIONAL
DISTRICT.

FOR EARLY NATIVE AMERICANS, THE SHEER SIZE OF TOTEM POLES AND OTHER SPIRIT-RELATED MONUMENTS —LIKE THIS TALL PIECE AT THE UNIVERSITY OF BRITISH COLUMBIA'S MUSEUM OF ANTHROPOLOGY— MUST HAVE BEEN INTIMIDATING.

IT'S DIFFICULT
ANYMORE TO FIND
ON-SITE EVIDENCE OF
WHAT CASCADIA'S
NATIVE AMERICAN
CULTURE WAS LIKE
BEFORE WHITES GAINED
CONTROL OF THE
REGION. BUT PIECES OF
ART MADE BY THE
EARLIEST INHABITANTS
AND MODERN USES OF
THEIR ARTISTIC STYLE
ARE ABUNDANT.
ABOVE:
BILL REID, A
VANCOUVER CARVER
AND SCULPTOR WHOSE
MOTHER WAS A HAIDA
INDIAN, HAS BECOME
FAMOUS FOR WORKS
SUCH AS *RAVEN AND
THE FIRST HUMANS*,
HOUSED IN THE
MUSEUM OF
ANTHROPOLOGY AT
THE UNIVERSITY OF
BRITISH COLUMBIA.
BELOW:
REID'S *THE JADE
CANOE* ATTRACTS
ATTENTION AT
VANCOUVER
INTERNATIONAL
AIRPORT.

ALTHOUGH TOTEM POLES CAN BE SEEN IN SEATTLE, CARVING THEM WAS NOT TRADITIONAL TO NATIVE AMERICANS LIVING AROUND PUGET SOUND. HOWEVER, IT WAS AN ART PRACTICED BY SEVERAL NATIVE GROUPS IN BRITISH COLUMBIA, INCLUDING THE HAIDAS OF THE QUEEN CHARLOTTE ISLANDS AND THE KWAKIUTL AND TSIMSHIAN PEOPLES OF THE PROVINCE'S SOUTHWEST CORNER. THEIR TOTEMIC ACCOMPLISHMENTS CAN STILL BE STUDIED AT STANLEY PARK AND OTHER GREENSWARDS AROUND VANCOUVER, AS WELL AS OUTSIDE SIMON FRASER UNIVERSITY'S MUSEUM OF ARCHAEOLOGY AND ETHNOLOGY, IN ADJACENT BURNABY, AND IN VICTORIA'S ROYAL BRITISH COLUMBIA MUSEUM, IN THUNDERBIRD PARK.

OPPOSITE:
KEEPING TRADITIONS ALIVE: ARTIST DAVID BOXELY FROM PORT LUDLOW, WASHINGTON, CARVES A TOTEM POLE IN THE TSIMSHIAN STYLE.

THE CAPITAL OF CAPITAL

Daphne Bramham

John ("Gassy Jack") Deighton didn't much like the look of the place when he arrived on the forested south shoulder of Burrard Inlet in late September 1867, just three years after the first international shipment of lumber had left the area for Australia. Writing to his brother Tom, still back in England, he described his new home as "a lonesome place…. Surrounded by Indians, I dare not look outdoors after dark. There was a friend of mine, about a mile distant, found with his head cut in two."

Of course, Jack wasn't exactly Prince Albert, either. Yes, with six dollars in his pocket, an Indian wife and a yellow dog in tow, and a barrel of whiskey as his most valuable possession, he had more than many other men roaming British Columbia in those depression years that followed the Fraser River gold rush. But it still amounted to pitifully little. What got him through was that barrel of firewater and his skills as a talker. (Legend has it that volubility earned Gassy Jack his nickname, rather than anything else you might imagine.) He set up a saloon in a twelve-by-twenty-foot shack on the inlet's muddy beach, and pretty soon he was thriving off parched workers from half a dozen nearby logging camps, two sawmills, and the docks where lumber was loaded for export. In his letters to Tom Deighton, Gassy Jack said it took about a year before anybody figured out his secret for success, and when they did, more saloons, hotels, and shops sprang up along the beach to further deprive laborers of their hard-earned income.

Within a short time, this ramshackle squatters' site came to be known as Gastown. More buildings were raised and folks poured in, including many Chinese, who had been brought to the West Coast to help build railways and eventually gathered in a flourishing community on Gastown's edge.

By 1887, when the final spike on the coast-to-coast Canadian Pacific Railway was driven at the edge of Burrard Inlet, the burg's prosperity was ensured. So was its future as a North American gateway to Asia, thanks in no small part to railroad visionary William Cornelius Van Horne, who had determined that the local port would be ideal for cargo ships sailing across the wide Pacific. A year later, the first inbound cargo—tea from China—arrived at newly renamed Vancouver.

More than a century has passed since then, and only now is Vancouver beginning to live up to the potential that Van Horne and others saw so long ago. However, even as it becomes a cosmopolitan center—the furthest financial capital of the Pacific Rim—it remains true to the entrepreneurial spirit and wild West character that Gassy Jack Deighton found so familiar.

Much of Vancouver's economic success comes from its geography. It is blessed with a sheltered deep-water port that just happens to be a full day closer to Asia by sea than are other West Coast seaports, such as San Francisco. Its airport offers the same advantage for travelers and goods bound for the far side of the Pacific. And, in this postindustrial age, even Vancouver's time zone weighs in its favor. As is true in Seattle, Vancouver businesspeople can talk with European contacts before the end of that continent's business day and to Asian contacts at the beginning of their workday.

The city has also enjoyed some good luck over the years. It was a going concern before it became the Canadian Pacific's western terminus. Vancouver lucked out again when it was chosen as the site of the 1986 world's fair, a little more than a decade before the British colony of Hong Kong was due to be returned to China.

As the Alaska-Yukon-Pacific Exposition of 1909 had introduced Seattle to the world, so Expo '86 (the World's Fair of 1986) was Vancouver's coming-out party. It not only marked the town's centennial, it also avouched its determination to become globally significant—a world-class city, if you don't find that term too egregious. Some locals objected to the long-term changes that the world's fair would bring to their quiescent village on the edge of the rain forest, their former Terminal City. But changes occurred anyway—on a huge scale.

Redevelopment of the fifty-block Expo site is one of the largest urban projects on the planet. Located beside False Creek, not too far from where Gassy Jack had his saloon, the property is under the control of another rags-to-riches entrepreneur. This entrepreneur happens to be one of Hong Kong's richest men—real estate tycoon Li Ka-shing—who is ponying up an estimated $3 billion to build a mix of commercial and residential towers. Li's decision to invest in Vancouver prompted other Hong Kong investors to do business in the city, and Canada's liberal immigration policies made them welcome. Under the investor-immigrant program, wealthy Hong Kong Chinese could exchange a $350,000 investment in British Columbia's Lower Mainland for a Canadian passport and a relatively safe and inexpensive city in which to buy a home (often a *huge* home, with plenty of space for future extended families). What's more, from Vancouver their new passport allowed them easy access to Hong Kong up until 1997—and even after that, as long as things work out all right under mainland Chinese control.

Some of these newcomers—such as Li's golfing partner Stanley Ho, who accumulated his billions running casinos in Macao—have spent their lucre conspicuously. Ho angered Vancouverites by purchasing a particularly visible piece of land at the entrance to Stanley Park and then building on it a mansion-away-from-home (with just enough retail space on its first floor to keep City Hall happy). While not exactly a rival to the high-tech bunker that Microsoft billionaire Bill Gates created overlooking Seattle's Lake Washington, Ho's multistory abode includes a garage with a turntable-like mechanism that guarantees he can drive off in whichever of his many cars he chooses without having to shuffle them in and out all the time.

Most deep-pocketed outsiders are less visible—though no less appreciated for the money they spread around.

Before Expo '86 was even a decade in the past, $2 billion had already been pumped into the Vancouver economy by immigrant investments. While Seattle has attracted a lot of its capital from Japan, Vancouver's Asian investors have hailed mainly from Hong Kong, with others streaming in from Taiwan, Korea, India, and

Southeast Asia. (There was even a rumor afloat in the mid-1990s that the multimillionaire sultan of Brunei had his eye on a $14 million waterfront mansion in West Vancouver, but, apparently, that was only wishful thinking on the part of local money-changers.) Specialty retail malls catering to Hong Kong Chinese, Taiwanese Chinese, and other Asians have sprung up across the city, making it possible now for those groups to do all their shopping in Cantonese, Mandarin, or Punjabi. The local media include two daily Chinese-language newspapers, a Chinese television station, and several Chinese-language radio stations. The annual Dragon Boat Festival, sponsored by Hongkong Bank of Canada, is one of the highlights of the spring season and features teams from every prominent business in the city.

The growth of Vancouver's stature on the world stage can't all be traced back to the fair, however. Since 1986, various levels of the Canadian and British Columbian governments have made regulatory modifications necessary to turn Vancouver into a nascent international financial center, an international maritime center, and a place where world disputes can be resolved.

In 1987, the city received its designation as an international financial center, putting it in the same category as Geneva, Zurich, Singapore, London, New York, and Tokyo. This designation means that Canadian and non-Canadian financial institutions operating in Vancouver are exempt from a significant number of federal and provincial taxes—as well as certain regulations—related to international transactions. But because it's all aimed at attracting wealthy individuals and companies from outside Canada with the promise of privacy, anonymity, and low taxes, these interests haven't been quick to proclaim their presence with glittering new downtown termitaries. Instead, since 1986, more than forty-eight discreet offices have opened in Greater Vancouver, bearing such prestigious names as the Swiss Bank Corporation, Credit Suisse, Sakura Bank, and the State Bank of India.

The one exception to this rule, the foreign-owned Hongkong Bank of Canada sports a tower and has its main office in Vancouver. A subsidiary of the Hongkong and Shanghai Bank, it chose British Columbia's largest city as its Canadian headquarters in 1988, when the homegrown Bank of B.C. fell on hard times and offered its branch network for sale. Although Hongkong Bank owes much of its strength to overseas capital, many Lower Mainlanders, distrustful of Canada's Toronto-based Big Five banks, rolled their accounts under its control after the Bank of B.C. finally went under. Others entrusted their money to the city's member-owned credit unions, one of which—Vancouver City Savings Credit Union, or VanCity, as it's better known—is now the third-largest credit union in Canada, with assets totaling nearly $4 billion (Canadian). Two of its competitors in town claim assets of more than $1 billion.

Further boosting Vancouver's economic profile was its 1991 naming as an international maritime center. Since then, more than twenty international shipping firms from Hong Kong, Taiwan, and the United States, together boasting assets of more than $5 billion, have moved their headquarters to Vancouver in order to take advantage of tax and regulatory breaks.

The city has even managed to make good news for itself out of bad global business news. Vancouver's International Commercial Arbitration Centre is one of only seven in the world to which companies and individuals can take their problems. Its

BRITISH CAPTAIN GEORGE VANCOUVER VISITED BOTH PUGET SOUND AND (SEEN HERE) VANCOUVER'S BURRARD INLET IN 1792. DURING HIS VISIT, HE WAS GREETED BY MANY CURIOUS NATIVE AMERICANS, WHO HAD NOT SEEN SHIPS AS LARGE AS VANCOUVER'S *DISCOVERY* AND *CHATHAM,* AND HE HAD THE CHANCE TO INSPECT THEIR VILLAGES AND WAYS OF LIFE. THE CAPTAIN MAGNANIMOUSLY NAMED MANY NATURAL LANDMARKS AFTER MEMBERS OF HIS CREW, BUT IT WOULD TAKE ANOTHER EIGHTY-SIX YEARS BEFORE BRITISH COLUMBIA'S PRINCIPAL CITY WOULD BE NAMED AFTER HIM. *COURTESY VANCOUVER PUBLIC LIBRARY, PHOTO NO. 8113*

particular expertise is the Pacific Rim, but since Canada signed the North American Free Trade Agreement in 1992, the center has also been involved in dispute resolution panels set up under NAFTA.

As was true in Gassy Jack's day, gold prospectors, loggers, and fishermen depend on Vancouver. Their goods are shipped from here, their earnings banked and spent here. But while forestry giants such as MacMillan Bloedel and big mining companies like Cominco and Placer Dome remain the principal drivers of the area's economy, increasingly the wealth is shifting to Jack's more rightful successors—those people inhabiting the service sector, whether in banking, tourism, software development, insurance, restaurants, film production, or just espresso delivery. The only other cities in North America with such a booming service economy are Orlando, Florida (home of Walt Disney World), and gambling-obsessed Las Vegas, Nevada.

The biggest business in town is now small business. You see its achievements everywhere, whether at the Vancouver Stock Exchange on Howe Street, among the elegant stores on Robson Street, in the trendy Latin quarter on Commercial Drive, or in one of suburban Richmond's four Asian shopping malls. Unlike Seattle, which has a heavy dependence on Boeing, Microsoft, Nordstrom, and Starbucks, more than

three-quarters of the businesses in Greater Vancouver count ten employees or fewer on their payrolls.

Jimmy Pattison, a dirt-poor boy from the Prairie provinces who came west and eventually opened a car dealership, is a leading example of someone who has turned service into a fortune. He now owns and controls the Jim Pattison Group, with sales of more than $3 billion (Canadian) a year in groceries, cars, paper products, magazines, neon signs, and a variety of other goods. His various businesses have made this trumpet-playing fundamentalist Christian so wealthy that when Frank Sinatra's mansion outside Palm Springs went up for sale, he bought it.

Not surprisingly, given the city's mild climate and leisure-loving inhabitants, many of Vancouver's new industries are related to fun and games. Marine technology companies have developed items ranging from single- and two-person submarines to a revolutionary Newt-suit for deep-water diving that has practical, military, and recreational applications. Ambitious thirty-somethings are designing snowboards for sale around the world and Vancouver-built mountain bikes rank among the international top sellers.

Speaking of fun, Vancouver is now the fourth most popular spot in North America for filmmaking (after Los Angeles, New York City, and Toronto). Since the industry got a toehold on Burrard Inlet in the mid-1980s, it has been expanding rapidly, largely on the strength of a weak Canadian dollar. Hardly any part of Greater Vancouver remains undiscovered and unfilmed. While Vancouverites aren't yet as blasé as Angelenos about stars like Kurt Russell showing up at the hockey rink to watch his son play, Katharine Hepburn sitting at a favorite coffee shop, or Robin Williams taking his turn at a local Yuk-Yuk's, Vancouverites no longer rubberneck themselves into traffic accidents every time they see a movie shooting on the streets of Gastown. They might not even recognize some of the stars these days, for even in the film industry, Vancouver thinks globally. Actors may come all the way from Hong Kong, Taiwan, and China to make movies on the Lower Mainland.

There are now more than six thousand Vancouver residents involved in the film and television industries, including those responsible for such animated works as the Emmy Award–winning *Ren and Stimpy* and MTV's controversial *Beavis and Butthead*.

If you think, however, that the raucous nineteenth-century Gastown days have vanished forever, that all we're left with is an era of cappuccino-drinking, Armani-suited yuppies, you obviously haven't heard of the Vancouver Stock Exchange.

The West Coast's only stock exchange was set up in 1907, in an ill-lit backroom on Pender Street. A so-called junior exchange, the VSE accounts for about one-third of all the money invested in Canada. Companies listed on the boards there are small, risky businesses desperately seeking to raise venture capital—and give you some *adv*enture in the meantime.

It's an exchange peopled by stock touts who, in the past, have not been above renting brass bands, hiring shapely bikini-clad models, and even bringing in live crocodiles as a way of focusing attention on their stocks. The stocks themselves can be no less bizarre. Of course, there have been great ones, such as the companies that developed the Hemlo and Eskay Creek goldfields using money raised here. Good technology companies have also gotten their start using money raised on the VSE. But so many ventures have received bad press (and maybe not bad enough) that Vancouver has been labeled the "Scam Capital of the World." Recall, for instance, the throat-spray appetite suppressant that not only made you eat less but freshened your breath at the same time, or the group that said it had a patent on a self-chilling beverage can. How about the company that claimed to be growing the planet's largest cultured pearls in a California shopping mall? Don't forget the people who asserted they were raising Brobdingnagian ostriches in—where else?—Texas. Another entrepreneur grew giant mutant rabbits in Nevada. More recently, an enterprise with a former Canadian prime minister on its board of directors was talking up a vending machine that deep-fried potato chips while you waited.

Gassy Jack Deighton, who died in 1875, would surely be perplexed by most of what Vancouver can offer these days—its cavernous new downtown library, SkyTrains whizzing by overhead, and skateboarders with neon coifs. But he'd recognize that kind of cowboying capitalism any day.

IN ONE OF THE LAST PICTURES TAKEN OF VANCOUVER BEFORE ITS 1886 FIRE, MEN CONGREGATE IN MAPLE TREE SQUARE, AT THE CORNER OF WATER AND CARRALL STREETS, TO DISCUSS POLITICS. A SIGN POSTED ON THE TREE ANNOUNCES THE CITY'S FIRST ELECTION, IN WHICH REAL-ESTATE DEALER MALCOLM MACLEAN RAN FOR MAYOR AGAINST RICHARD ALEXANDER, A MILL OWNER. ONLY WHITE MEN WERE ALLOWED TO VOTE IN THE ELECTION, WHICH MACLEAN WON—BUT PERHAPS NOT HONESTLY (MANY OF HIS SUPPORTERS ALLEDGEDLY CAST MORE THAN ONE BALLET). THIS AREA IS NOW PART OF GASTOWN. COURTESY VANCOUVER PUBLIC LIBRARY, PHOTO NO. 1093

HEAR THAT LONESOME
WHISTLE BLOW! THE
ROYAL HUDSON STEAM
LOCOMOTIVE CHUGS
INTO THE TOWN OF
SQUAMISH, BRITISH
COLUMBIA, AT THE END
OF ITS DAILY THREE-
HOUR-LONG JOURNEY
FROM THE SHADOW OF
THE LIONS GATE
BRIDGE IN NORTH
VANCOUVER. OUTSIDE
SQUAMISH, SIGHTSEERS
MAY TAKE IN SHANNON
FALLS—AT 1,100 FEET
(340 METERS), THE
PROVINCE'S THIRD-
HIGHEST WATERFALL.

OPPOSITE:
LAKE UNION, JUST
NORTH OF DOWNTOWN
SEATTLE, IS THE
LAUNCHING PAD
FOR KENMORE
AIR FLOATPLANES,
CARRYING PASSENGERS
NORTH TO
WASHINGTON'S SAN
JUAN ISLANDS.

CASCADIA NO LONGER
DEPENDS SOLELY ON
SHIPS FOR ITS TRADE
AND TRANSPORTATION,
YET ITS PORTS REMAIN
BUSY.

ABOVE:
CRAFT OF ALL SIZES
AND SORTS—SOME OF
THEM CAUSING YOU TO
LOOK TWICE AND EVEN
DOUBLE-CHECK THE
YEAR—CAN BE
SPOTTED ALONG THE
SEATTLE WATERFRONT.
BELOW:
FERRIES REMAIN THE
PRINCIPAL MODE OF
TRAVEL BETWEEN
MAINLAND WASHINGTON
AND SAN JUAN ISLANDS
TOWNS, SUCH AS
FRIDAY HARBOR.

ABOVE:
CRUISE SHIPS ARE A
COMMON SIGHT OFF THE
COAST OF VANCOUVER.
BELOW:
EVEN THE OCCASIONAL
STERN-WHEELER CAN
BE SPOTTED CHURNING
UP THE WATERS NEAR
SEATTLE'S UNIVERSITY
OF WASHINGTON.

ABOVE:

THE WASHINGTON
STATE FERRY SYSTEM
IS THE LARGEST IN THE
UNITED STATES,
CARRYING SOME 18
MILLION PASSENGERS
A YEAR OVER NINE
ROUTES. BUSIEST ON
WEEKDAYS IS THE
25-MINUTE RUN WEST
FROM SEATTLE TO
BAINBRIDGE ISLAND,
A WOODED UPPER-
MIDDLE-CLASS RETREAT
ON THE OTHER SIDE OF
PUGET SOUND.

BELOW:

CARGO SHIPS AFLOAT IN
PUGET SOUND REMIND
SEATTLEITES THAT
THEY LIVE IN ONE OF
AMERICA'S BUSIEST
HARBORS, HANDLING
ELECTRONICS,
AUTOMOBILES, FOREST
PRODUCTS, AND OTHER
GOODS BEING TRADED
BETWEEN THE UNITED
STATES AND EXPANDING
MARKETS IN ASIA.

THE *VICTORIA HARBOUR FERRY* HELPS BOTH LOCALS AND VISITORS TO BETTER APPRECIATE VANCOUVER'S WATERFRONT SIGHTS— FROM THE WATERLINE UP.

OVERLEAF: LOGS FLOATING OUTSIDE A WASHINGTON MILL WAIT TO BE CUT UP FOR LUMBER, EITHER FOR USE IN THE STATES OR FOR SHIPMENT ABROAD. DESPITE CONCERNS OVER DIMINISHING NATURAL RESOURCES, CASCADIA HAS BEEN SELLING ITS PLENTIFUL TIMBER TO THE WORLD FOR MORE THAN A CENTURY AND A HALF.

PAGES 166–67: LOOKING IMPOSSIBLY YELLOW AGAINST THE MOUNTAINS SURROUNDING VANCOUVER, A SULFUR PILE AWAITS TRANSPORT.

LIKE SEATTLE, THE
PORT OF VANCOUVER
WAS EARLY TO SEE
THE POTENTIAL OF
CONTAINER TRANSPORT,
AND HAS SINCE
PROSPERED.
ABOVE:
A CONTAINER SHIP
READIES ITS
DEPARTURE FROM THE
CITY'S VANTERM
CENTRAL PIER, IN THE
SHADOW OF GROUSE
MOUNTAIN, A SKI AREA
SURPRISINGLY
CONVENIENT TO
DOWNTOWN.
BELOW:
CRANES LOOM LIKE
GARISH MECHANICAL
MONSTERS OVER
THE CARGO WAITING
TO BE MOVED OFF
VANCOUVER'S
WATERFRONT.

EVEN THE 76-STORY
COLUMBIA SEAFIRST
CENTER, SEATTLE'S
TALLEST BUILDING (ON
THE FAR RIGHT), LOOKS
PUNY WHEN SEEN
BEHIND THE MAMMOTH
MACHINERY THAT'S
RESPONSIBLE FOR
UNLOADING CARGO AT
THE CITY'S DOCKS.

OVERLEAF:
WILLIAM BOEING, THE
HEIR TO A MIDWESTERN
LUMBER FORTUNE,
STARTED TO BUILD
AIRPLANES IN 1916.
BY WORLD WAR II,
THANKS IN LARGE PART
TO FEDERAL DEMAND
FOR MILITARY
AIRCRAFT, BOEING'S
COMPANY HAD BECOME
AN INDUSTRIAL GIANT.
TODAY, IT IS ONE OF
CASCADIA'S LARGEST
EMPLOYERS,
PRODUCING 747S AND
OTHER PLANES FOR A
WIDE VARIETY OF
NATIONAL AND
INTERNATIONAL
CLIENTS. ITS PLANT AT
EVERETT, WASHINGTON,
HAS THE LARGEST
SPACE UNDER ONE
ROOF IN THE WORLD.

PAGES 172–73:
AT THE MICROSOFT
CAMPUS IN REDMOND,
WASHINGTON, CEO BILL
GATES AND HIS FELLOW
COMPUTER VISIONARIES
ARE NOT ONLY HELPING
TO CREATE TODAY'S
"INFORMATION
SUPERHIGHWAY" BUT
ENSURING THAT THE
NEXT GENERATION OF
CASCADIANS WILL BE
READY TO NAVIGATE ITS
MANY INTRICATE LANES.

POSTCARDS FROM THE NORTHWEST EDGE

Brenda Peterson

Imagine that you are here with me on the windswept, sibilant shores of Puget Sound. It is high tide and the late summer light slants along the waves to make a shining path, which the old amphibian in me longs to follow across the water—if only my land legs could remember the balance and flow of tail and gill.

This inland sea is serpentine, embracing our islands and peninsulas like a green dragon that coils north from Seattle, entwines its fresh water with the salty straits of Georgia and Juan de Fuca, and finally comes to lick at the docks of Vancouver and Victoria. Cascadians have always been water folk, shaped by this Sound and also by the sounds of rivers and rains. The stories Northwest Coast natives first told were of sea creatures and underwater tribes that could "shape-shift" into humans. The stories we still tell are syncopated with the rhythms of tide and wind, the cries of seagulls, eagles, and great blue herons, the whooshing breath of whales and distant foghorns.

Our abundant, defining coast holds us together with its cadences of water and weather. Sometimes we feel so hidden by marine fog and darkening showers that we wonder if our far-off territory is truly isolated from the remaining, mostly landlocked sprawl of North America. But when we try to spell out our "rainy day people" intimacies to outsiders, they cannot believe that we actually *enjoy* living for many months of each year aswirl in great, flowing gowns of gray mist. I describe for my East Coast friends our subtle shades of winter—from gloaming skies of "high gray" to "low gray" with violet streaks like the water's delicate aura—and they wonder if my brain has, indeed, become waterlogged.

Perhaps the best way to make outsiders understand life here is to send out a few postcards, as world travelers of yore sent postcards home to explain the customs and vistas of foreign territories. What follows, then, are three portraits of Cascadians and this place we share—each one a tiny window through our mystical rain and into our watery souls.

One summer morning as I sat in my small waterfront studio, behind my old teak desk—I imagine it as a sturdy ship sailing me out over spacious Puget Sound—I suddenly noticed a stream of sickly white runoff spewing into the clear waves. A chalky cloud bloomed on the beach, and all the seabirds scattered with calls of alarm. I ran out into the hallway to find my neighbors already on the alert.

"The Department of Energy and King County Parks both say they'll send someone out here within the hour," my neighbor Lisa called as she manned the phone. Her husband, Victor, and I, along with our apartment manager, Bill, clambered over giant driftwood to the beach, where we found a sickening sight: filmy white rivulets entering Puget Sound through a wide culvert.

"Oh, no," said Victor, "this is where the otters swim down to fish on the beach." He scooped up a sample of the unnatural runoff and scowled. "Looks really toxic," he breathed. We both followed Bill's gaze up the hillside, trying to track the watershed.

"Construction," Bill groaned, nodding to a new house halfway up the slope. "Let's check it out."

Victor found the culprit: a painting contractor who was washing gallons of white paint into a stream uphill from our beach. He and Bill walked directly up to the guy. "You know, sir," Victor began, in his soft schoolteacher's voice, "the paint you're dumping into this little creek is polluting the stream and spilling down into the Sound itself."

"Oh," the contractor said, looking abashed but not ashamed. "I was just washing out my truck, where I spilled some…uh, paint."

Victor paused as if figuring out how to teach this adult a lesson that every one of his schoolchildren knew by heart. Then Bill, a geologist who could also double as a wrestler, looked the painter squarely in the eye and said quietly, "No, sir. That paint's been flowing for over two hours. You should see what a mess you've made in the Sound."

The contractor turned away, at last a bit chagrined. "Oh, well, it's not oil-base…" and he faded off. At least he stopped dumping the paint.

Later, as we waited on the beach below for the last of the pale trail to trickle out of the culvert, watching the white cloud spill foam and filter into the waves, we wondered how many of our neighbors that contractor had polluted, casually and with no sense of connection to our natural waterways. Here in Cascadia, these fragile, intricate watershed systems still spawn precious salmon, nourish backyard gardens, and shelter great blue herons. A toxic spill can be disastrous. Could the paint, we worried, have poisoned the river otters that frequented our culvert?

As it turned out, our fears were relieved. The next week I sat on my backyard beach with my friend Marlene, who was born and reared on these shores. Suddenly we heard a swoosh and a thump and then saw a small otter, its dark fur slick and gleaming, hopping on its belly and back flippers across barnacles and rocks to glide gracefully into the Sound. We heard it chitter and splash before it suddenly dived, coming up with a flat flounder flapping between its teeth. We clapped and the otter studied us briefly, then hopped back up the beach, pausing to shake out its fur before disappearing into the culvert, the live fish still struggling to escape.

I watched happily as the otter swam upstream through the same pipe that had so recently spilled paint. When I told Marlene about the encounter between my neighbors and the contractor, she said, "They're local heroes, aren't they? They're what neighborliness and the Northwest are all about."

As I watch our region struggle to balance conservation of its natural beauty with the demands of growth and greed, I think about my friend's words. And I hope that the local hero in all of us here will continue to stop the spills and protect the marine life and teach our next generations the lessons that make the natural world such a dear companion.

Not long ago, I went to see the friends in Vancouver who had first taught me how to sail. Arriving at their houseboat on the Fraser River flats, I was not surprised to find their Boston Whaler equipped with a banquet, life preservers, and binoculars. Lynettie Sue and her nautical husband, David, had planned a daytrip for us across the Strait of Georgia to tiny Gossip Island. On the way, they hoped we would spot some orcas (killer whales).

Above the roar of the boat's motor, we sang selections from Broadway musicals and greeted some of my friends' neighbors in other boats. We saw no pods of beautifully breaching orcas, but we were surrounded by sea lions and seals, otters and eagles.

Fewer than one hundred people, I discovered, occupy Gossip Island. Only a minority of these live on the island year-round. Fiercely rooted, the islanders share in maintaining the island's welfare. The rest are summer residents from Victoria or Vancouver. Our destination was the home of one such seasonal dweller: biologist-writer Stefani Paine, author of *The Nature of Sea Otters* and former manager of public affairs at the Vancouver Aquarium. Now a part-time Victorian, Paine was the only woman on the American–Canadian Salmon Commission. She told us stories of the dangers facing Cascadia's premier fish, making it clear that while Canada and the United States haggle over quotas and fishing rights, the salmon are dying out.

Dwindling seafood populations are no small matter in an area that built much of its history on fishing. As Native Americans tell it, salmon were so plentiful here just a century ago that people could actually walk across small rivers by balancing on the backs of their spawning multitudes. These cold-blooded vertebrates played such a significant role in Northwest native life that they became part of local legend. Myths teach that there is a balance between land and sea that must be honored. To maintain this equipoise, certain inhabitants of the land—the Salmon People—would volunteer to exchange places with their salmon kin every fishing season, thus assuring the survival of both humans and nonhumans. This web of life, this great circle of being, was organized not by the food chain hierarchy that we learn about in earth-science courses but by the cycle of birth and death intermingled.

Salmon emphasize the importance of this cycle every time they die naturally, for in death their bodies—desiccated from the heroic last swim home—spawn another generation. If these fish today are not completing their circle of regeneration, what meaning does that have for the earth's future and humankind's next generations? What will happen if the Salmon People lose their salmon?

What I learned in talking with Stefani Paine about her work with the salmon commission was both bleak and bracing. Half in jest, she suggested at one point that Cascadian fishers be allowed to take all the salmon they could find—with no limits—instead of slowly and painfully depleting our once great sea brethren. Sometimes she thinks our salmon are already certifiably extinct and that what we're seeing now in stores are just the few survivors struggling toward an inevitable end. Eventually, she concluded, "We'll be like the East Coast: salmon gone." As she said this, an eagle flew overhead, its scream reaching us as loneliness and loss.

Back on my home shore, I thought about Paine's prophecy while watching a new season's flotilla of fishers bob over the Alki Point salmon runs. What I was seeing, I mused, was the result of a broken treaty between ourselves and the natural world. We have taken more from the Salmon People than we have given back; because of that, the salmon are not returning to their spawning grounds. As an indicator species that signals the health of our ecosystem, the salmon predict the human future. Our fates are inexorably linked; if the salmon die, then we, too, will suffer a decline.

I found myself praying as I imagined human tribes have prayed for centuries on Puget Sound—praying for the salmon's survival. I finally lit a candle and burned some lavender out there on the beach, in sight of the armada, calling all the while upon any spirits that might still protect the salmon and these shores.

Chief Sealth, the visionary and leader for whom Seattle was named, once said, "Our dead never forget the beautiful world which gave them being...and ever yearn in tender, fond affection over the lonely hearted living, and often return to visit, console, and comfort them." The Salmon People, both human and fish folk, need some comfort these days—and more self-control. Can we stop decimating the salmon long enough to help restore their runs? Can we honor our pact to balance what we take from the Northwest's bounty with our efforts to preserve that bounty? Our identity depends on it.

I will never forget a luminous Christmas Eve celebration here on the banks of Puget Sound. It was a moment that, for me, will always define both the hope of a new year and the prospect of reciprocity between humans and nature.

The tide was low and the moon full when hundreds of people huddled together in circles around a bonfire on Alki Beach. Our spirits and breaths were made visible in bright puffs as we sang "Angels We Have Heard on High." Our faces glowed in the firelight, our boots sank deep into wet winter sand. Though the night was freezing, we sang out "Glor-or-or-or-or-or-ria!" with the waves in perfect pitch.

I wondered then if any sea lions raised their bewhiskered snouts to listen to our glad song. Were porpoises or whales passing on their migration to winter breeding grounds trying to decipher our gleeful vocalizations? Did the jellyfish and seals float a little easier near our shores because we were singing to them? How long had it been since an entire tribe of people made joyful noises of song on this stretch of sand?

How lonely we humans are, singing our hallelujahs in cramped churches when the whole natural world is listening and singing back—in waves, in birdcalls, in thunder and wind. Every tree breathes a different song when the breezes stir its branches—from the low elegy of old-growth cedar to the trembling treble whispers of alder and aspen. And every land has its own music.

Along the Cascadian coast, I hope we can continue to make music in a balanced harmony between human and animal, between our species and the sea, between our land life and the spirit life that lives beside us. I send out these small postcards not only to provide glimpses of life here but also as part of a greater song that continually seeks nature's healing harmonies, a true counterpoint to our human voices.

THE YOUNG AND THE RESTLESS

Laurel Wellman

Cascadians, inhabiting one of the world's great recreational paradises, tend to pin their identities to what they do on weekends. And, not surprisingly, this regional love of leisure is a very big deal with the young and the trend-conscious.

Back when I was attending high school in a Vancouver suburb, kids would self-consciously leave their ski-lift tickets dangling from their jacket zippers after a weekend spent on the slopes of the Coast Mountains. The quantity and origins of these tattered tags revealed a great deal about the coolness of their owners. Grouse Mountain tickets rated higher than those from Seymour Mountain, which were better than those from Cypress Bowl. But stubs brought back from Whistler and Blackcomb, the expensive resorts ninety minutes north of the city—those were the real trump cards.

I mentioned this recently to a younger friend, and she told me that the ante has since been upped. "Only *losers* have day tickets," she said, a little patronizingly. "All the cool people have season passes."

In Cascadia, where the cult of leisure has developed to such a degree that even junior-high school students rate the subtle gradations in lift-ticket status with a reflex snobbery, it often seems that everyone under the age of thirty is required to have fun. Certainly that's what the outside media would have people believe. They've touted Pacific Northwest's low-stress, high-activity life-style with such fervor and frequency that inhabitants of more conventional metropolises must question how, what with our supposedly packed schedules of sailing lessons and craft-beer tastings, we get any work done at all. No wonder Torontonians, echoing something that Rudyard Kipling wrote about Vancouver after his visit in 1899—"Such a land is good for an energetic man. It is also not so bad for the loafer"—mock the city on Burrard Inlet as "Lotus Land." From the shores of Lake Ontario or the Hudson River, Cascadia must look very like Eden with slugs instead of snakes.

But if young Cascadians aren't living the good life at all moments, it's not for lack of opportunities. Seattle and Vancouver offer wide ranges of recreational pursuits—including hiking, windsurfing, rock climbing, in-line skating, and cycling—as well as mild climates that make it possible to play outdoors year-round. Both towns claim lively music-club and coffee-bar scenes, as well as lots of chic taverns and brew pubs catering to a youthful clientele. So if it's social death in your crowd to be caught without a season pass, there's still a good chance that you'll find a comfortable milieu here. You just have to cultivate some conspicuous leisure pursuit, even if it's nothing more energetic than attending poetry readings.

Perhaps it's to be expected that the people most prepared to appreciate this area's opportunities are those who are newest to them. Take Andrew Chan, for instance. At twenty-seven years of age, he has lived in Vancouver for less than a year since immigrating from Hong Kong. He has already decided that this city will be his permanent home. "I love it here," he told me. "The surroundings are beautiful. There's a large area for living—in Hong Kong, it's very crowded." Chan spends many of his off-hours walking the seawall at Stanley Park. Or he'll head south to the community of White Rock, where he enjoys the broad, sandy beach fronting Semiahmoo Bay. If he's feeling homesick, he swings by Vancouver's extensive Chinatown, where three or four bookstores supply him with news from the far side of the Pacific.

In the early 1990s it might have seemed as though everyone between the ages of fifteen and thirty was wearing plaid flannel and Doc Martens, spending days hanging out in cafés and nights bounding around mosh pits. But the Generation-X slacker was more a citizen of MTV and Hollywood than of Cascadia.

The cliché ignored this region's deepening ethnic diversity, the heavy influx of Asian immigrants like Andrew Chan. It also ignored economic realities. Being a serious slacker isn't easy in Vancouver or Seattle, where even the young have benefited from recent boom times. Surely one of the supreme ironies of our era is that some of the more affluent among Cascadia's leisure-loving youth class—those who could best afford to take a few days off to, say, attend Washington's annual Skagit Valley Tulip Festival or go kayaking up the west coast of Vancouver Island—have found themselves with virtually no leisure hours at all.

Ethan O'Connor is a prime example. A program manager at Microsoft Corporation, the Seattle area's software giant, he has framed his life tightly around the wired culture. "It's definitely a distinct universe," he explained. "I don't feel part of the whole so-called Seattle scene." He hasn't room for it on his calendar, anyway; by his own admission, O'Connor spends twelve hours a day at his office, leaving him little chance to test out the ski slopes or join the running crowd at Green Lake. Even if he did find some extra hours, he might still feel out of place in his city, for, as he confessed, "I can't stand coffee. I drink Pepsi."

Hired right out of college, O'Connor is now twenty-five, married, the owner of a condo, and a stockholder in one of America's most profitable companies, while other people his age only dream about stability. Microsoft employs thousands of men and women just like him. Yet, he said, when he does get out to a nightclub, the people he meets don't relate easily to him. "They're like, 'What are you doing here? You should be out spending a million dollars buying Leonardo da Vinci prints or something.'"

But O'Connor represents a new reality in Cascadia. It used to be that twenty-somethings here were more willing to trade a certain degree of career advancement for some quality downtime. Nowadays, it seems Cascadians are anxious to immerse themselves entirely in business early on, when they're still full of new and bright ideas, with the hope that they won't burn out before they can reap the rewards of their genius and finally relax.

What scant freedom O'Connor allows himself he spends in shopping Seattle's many used-book stores, looking for the vintage Hardy Boys mysteries he collects. The odds are good that he can be spotted at Twice-Told Tales atop Capitol Hill.

In Cascadia, where you hang out is almost as important as what you do there. The Capitol Hill neighborhood is certainly one of the most fashionable draws. Very urban, with a substantial gay and lesbian residency, it's thick with apartment structures and old mansions, innovative restaurants, art-film theaters, and lively clubs such as

Moe's Mo'roc'can Café. It's also home to *The Stranger*, the weekly entertainment guide that's devoured by Seattle scene-makers.

While you're on the prowl for other hubs of hipness, don't miss Fremont, just to the northwest of Capitol Hill, across Lake Union. On most pleasant days, the streets there are packed with people visiting breweries, vintage kitsch emporia, and public artworks. On weekends, they flock to the local flea market, presided over by a huge and controversial bronze statue of Lenin, purchased from the former Soviet Union. Evenings invite "Fremonsters" to bring their own chairs and popcorn and watch films being screened against the side of a building at the market site.

Head east and you'll hit another major youth zone: the U District, that student ghetto that surrounds the University of Washington. Along University Avenue—or just "The Ave," as most Seattleites know it—cluster coffeeterias, used-record outlets, inexpensive eateries, and a twenty-four-hour photocopying center where students pulling all-nighters are known to allay some of their anxiety by Xeroxing various essential body parts.

In Vancouver, the University of British Columbia is surrounded by some of the most expensive single-family housing in the city. So the student district has moved east, and Vancouver's equivalent to The Ave is a stretch of Commercial Drive centered on the city's most famous coffeehouse: Joe's. Before there was Starbucks, Joe's was where many young Vancouverites tasted their first cappuccinos. And the Drive, with its studied Bohemian ambiance, might also have been the place where they first shopped for vintage clothing or bought an imported CD.

Slightly older and more affluent Vancouverites patronize Yaletown, a former warehouse district at downtown's southeast corner. This is really less a residential area than a hangout, boasting more upscale pool halls than any other quarter of the city. During the day, Yaletown bustles with shoppers and office drones, but in the moonlight, club- and restaurant-goers compete for the neighborhood's scarce parking slots, and the well-heeled keep joints such as Bar None and the Yaletown Brewing Company—both of which feature pool tables—hopping.

The pull Cascadia exerts on the young and ambitious is the same as the pull of boomtowns everywhere, and the promise of jobs and money is enough to lure many to Seattle and Vancouver. But newcomers to the area—whether they are from Hong Kong, Toronto, or Los Angeles—quickly find that here they are expected to pursue play with the same intensity as they do their careers. To do less would be, well, ungrateful, maybe even treasonous. Allegiance to Cascadia's code demands, after all, knowing where your lift ticket is from.

RAIN KEEPS CASCADIANS HOLED UP IN THEIR HOMES FOR MUCH OF THE YEAR, SO WHEN THE SUN FINALLY BREAKS THROUGH, THEY CLOG THE STREETS. HERE, YOUNG MEN AND WOMEN, DRAPED IN A KIND OF NOUVEAU RADICAL—THRIFT STORE CHIC, KEEP THE STREETSCAPE HOPPING ON SEATTLE'S CROWDED CAPITOL HILL.

OVERLEAF: AT ALMOST ANY HOUR OF THE DAY, PEOPLE CAN BE SEEN AT SEATTLE'S GREEN LAKE PARK, FISHING, OR KAYAKING, OR JUST HANGING OUT ON PIERS CONTEMPLATING THE STATE OF THE WORLD.

PREVIOUS PAGES:
THE UNIVERSITY OF
WASHINGTON, FOUNDED
IN 1861, NOW HAS A
35,000 STUDENT BODY
AND A TREMENDOUS
NUMBER OF ALUMNI—
MANY OF WHOM SHOW
UP EACH SEASON TO
WATCH THE HUSKIES
FOOTBALL TEAM
(ALSO KNOWN AS
"THE DAWGS") PLAY
AT HUSKY STADIUM.

PERHAPS BECAUSE IT
RAINS SO OFTEN IN
CASCADIA, RESIDENTS
OF THE REGION ARE
AGGRESSIVE FAIR-
WEATHER SPORTS
PARTICIPANTS.

ABOVE:
THE COURTS CROWD UP
FAST AT THE SEATTLE
TENNIS CLUB, WHERE
PLAYERS CAN LOOK OUT
ON LAKE WASHINGTON
AND THE BELLEVUE
SUBURBS IN BETWEEN
VOLLEYS.
BELOW:
IT OBVIOUSLY
TAKES GREAT
CONCENTRATION—AND
A HEALTHY WARDROBE
OF WHITES—TO BE A
STAR AT VANCOUVER'S
TERMINAL CITY LAWN
BOWLING CLUB.

ABOVE:
LOOK MA, NO SKATES! FIELD-HOCKEY PLAYERS CHARGE OVER THE ARTIFICIAL TURF AT ANDY LIVINGSTON PARK, ON THE RECENTLY REDEVELOPED FORMER EXPO '86 FAIRGROUNDS IN VANCOUVER.

BELOW:
FAMED DESIGNER ROBERT TRENT JONES II IS RESPONSIBLE FOR THE CHATEAU WHISTLER GOLF CLUB, AT WHISTLER, BRITISH COLUMBIA.

BLACKCOMB MOUNTAIN, AT WHISTLER, BRITISH COLUMBIA, PROVIDES SOME OF CASCADIA'S BEST SKIING DURING WINTER MONTHS. IN SUMMER, THOUGH, THE VISITORS IT ATTRACTS HAVE OTHER SPORTING PLEASURES IN MIND. OPPOSITE: HORSEBACK RIDERS TROT IN THE SHADOW OF IDLED SKI LIFTS. RIGHT: AN ENTIRELY DIFFERENT BREED OF SPEED ENTHUSIASTS— SKATEBOARDERS— PRACTICES AT THE BASE OF BLACKCOMB.

A HAIR-RAISING
EXPERIENCE, INDEED:
SNOWBOARD RACERS
COMPETE AT
BLACKCOMB MOUNTAIN,
NEAR WHISTLER,
BRITISH COLUMBIA.

RESIDENTS OF WASHINGTON AND BRITISH COLUMBIA WHO DO NOT SKI ARE LOOKED ON WITH SOME SKEPTICISM. IT'S NORMAL FOR LOCALS TO HIT THE CASCADE SLOPES IN WINTER, SEARCHING FOR THE FASTEST RUNS, THE DEEPEST POWDER, AND THE MOST COLORFUL APRÈS-SKI VENUES.

OVERLEAF: RESIDENTS OF ADVENTURES WEST RESORT DEMONSTRATE THEIR ICE HOCKEY PROWESS ON ALTA LAKE, IN THE VALLEY BENEATH BRITISH COLUMBIA'S WHISTLER MOUNTAIN.

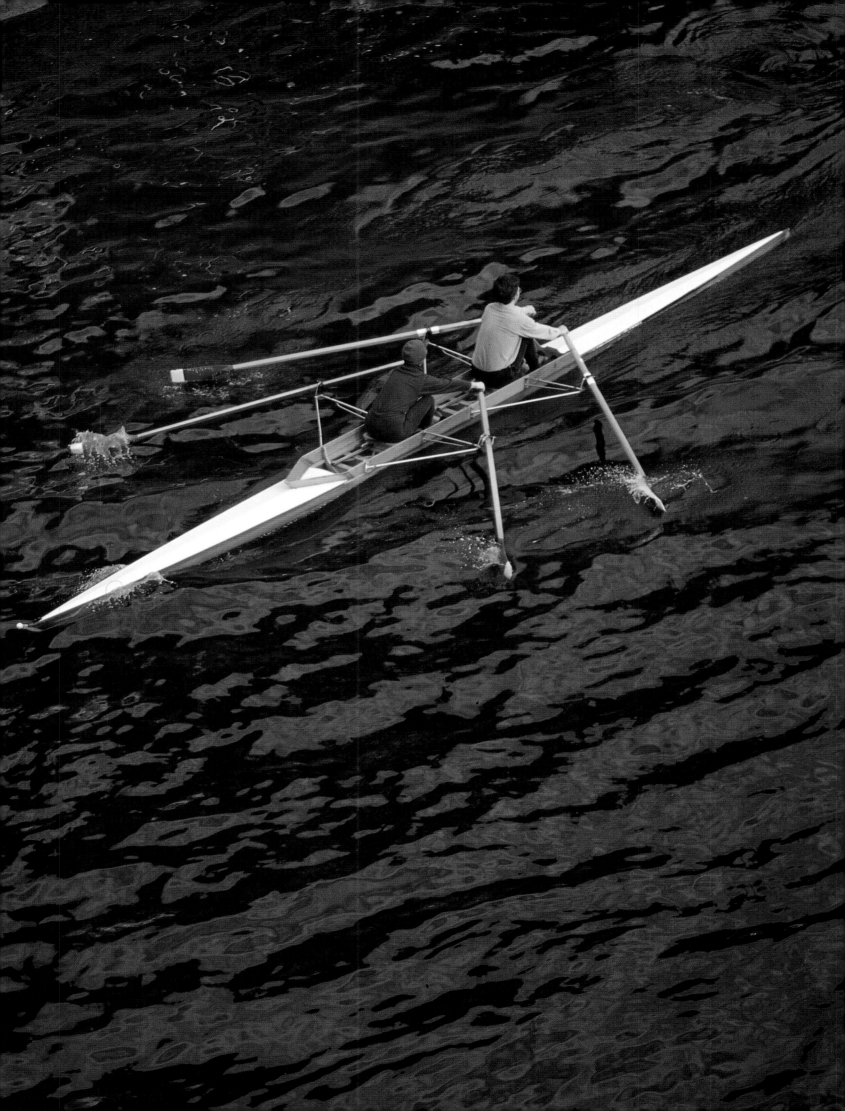

THE SERENITY OF
ROWING SEEMS
TO APPEAL GREATLY
TO CASCADIANS.
OPPOSITE:
TWO-PERSON SCULLS
ARE OFTEN SEEN
PLYING THE WATERS OF
SEATTLE'S UNION BAY.
RIGHT:
KAYAKERS HEAD OFF
INTO ROCHE HARBOR
FROM THE HOTEL
DE HARO, ON
WASHINGTON'S SAN
JUAN ISLAND.
THE HOTEL WAS BUILT
IN THE 1880S BY
JOHN MCMILLIN, WHO
OWNED A HUGE AND
PROSPEROUS LIME KILN
ON THE ISLAND AND
NEEDED A PLACE TO
HOUSE DISTINGUISHED
GUESTS—LIKE
THEODORE ROOSEVELT.

VICTORIA'S DRAGON
BOAT FESTIVAL, HELD
IN MID-AUGUST, IS A
MULTICULTURAL EVENT
THAT FEATURES
ENERGETIC DRAGON
BOAT RACES THROUGH
THE INNER HARBOUR.
THE RACES ARE
SUPPOSED TO BE BASED
ON CHINESE LEGEND.

EVERY AUGUST,
SEATTLE'S LAKE
WASHINGTON HOSTS
AN UNLIMITED
HYDROPLANE
EXTRAVAGANZA. A
PRINCIPAL FEATURE OF
SEAFAIR, THE CITY'S
CELEBRATION OF ITS
MARITIME HERITAGE,
THE RACES TURN STAN
SAYRES MEMORIAL
PARK—THE PREMIER
VIEWING SPOT—INTO A
CONFUSION OF NOISE,
WARM BEER, AND
PROVOCATIVELY
EXPOSED FLESH.
ABOVE:
HYDROPLANES EXECUTE
A LONG OVAL IN THE
LAKE, WITH
STRAIGHTAWAYS
PARALLELING THE
SHORELINE.
BELOW:
WINNERS AND FAMILIAR
RACERS ARE NOT SHY
ABOUT WAVING HELLO
TO THEIR FANS.

SAILORS ENJOY
SOME OF THE MOST
MAGNIFICENT VIEWS IN
CASCADIA, WHETHER
OF THE MOUNTAINS
AROUND BRITISH
COLUMBIA'S ALTA LAKE
(LEFT) OR THE
DOWNTOWN SEATTLE
SKYLINE, SEEN FROM
LAKE UNION (OPPOSITE).

OVERLEAF:
RESIDENTS OF
SEATTLE'S QUEEN ANNE
HILL HAVE AN ENVIABLE
VIEW OF THE SEASONAL
"DUCK DODGE" RACES,
HELD ON LAKE UNION.

IN SEATTLE, YOU'RE NEVER FAR FROM A PIZZA PLACE THAT DELIVERS. THIS AQUATIC DOOR-TO-BOAT DECK SERVICE WAS AVAILABLE FOR A SEAFAIR BOAT GATHERING ON LAKE UNION.

OPPOSITE:
FIBERGLASS SEACRAFT MAY BE FINE FOR SOME PEOPLE, BUT MANY SEATTLEITES PREFER TO FLOAT ON WOOD, THANK YOU VERY MUCH. THE CENTER FOR WOODEN BOATS, AT THE SOUTH END OF LAKE UNION, SERVES AS A HISTORICAL CENTER AND HOST TO ENTRIES IN REGULAR WOODEN BOAT SHOWS, SUCH AS THE *DILIGENCE*.

OVERLEAF:
JARRET MORTON AND HIS DOG ROW TO SCHOOL FROM HIS HOUSEBOAT HOME ON ECHO BAY, IN BRITISH COLUMBIA.

PAGES 206–7:
FROM THE WOODED SUBURB OF MERCER ISLAND, EAST OF SEATTLE, THE SUN IN ITS DESCENT IS RATHER REMINISCENT OF THE MOON IN ITS RISE.

DILIGENCE
SEATTLE